APPALACHIAN MOUNTAIN CHRISTIANITY

GEORGE H. SHRIVER
LECTURE SERIES IN
RELIGION IN
AMERICAN HISTORY

NO. 10

APPALACHIAN MOUNTAIN CHRISTIANITY

THE SPIRITUALITY OF OTHERNESS

Bill J. Leonard

THE UNIVERSITY
OF GEORGIA PRESS
Athens

© 2024 by the University of Georgia Press
Athens, Georgia 30602
www.ugapress.org
All rights reserved
Set in 11/15 Adobe Caslon by Rebecca A. Norton

Most University of Georgia Press titles are
available from popular e-book vendors.

Printed digitally

Library of Congress Cataloging-in-Publication Data
Names: Leonard, Bill (Bill J.) author
Title: Appalachian mountain Christianity :
the spirituality of otherness / Bill J. Leonard.
Description: Athens : The University of Georgia Press, [2024] |
Series: George H. Shriver lecture series in religion in American
history ; no. 10 | Includes bibliographical references and index.
Identifiers: LCCN 2024010588 | ISBN 9780820367262 pdf |
ISBN 9780820367255 epub | ISBN 9780820367248 paperback |
ISBN 9780820367125 hardback
Subjects: LCSH: Primitive Baptists—Appalachian Region—History |
Marginality, Social—Appalachian Region—History |
Pentecostalism—Appalachian Region—History |
Universalism—Appalachian Region—History
Classification: LCC BX6383 .L36 2024 |
DDC 286/.4—dc23/eng/20240827
LC record available at https://lccn.loc.gov/2024010588

In gratitude for and in memory of
the Reverend Dr. Mary Lee Daugherty,
Dr. Helen Matthews Lewis,
the Reverend Pauline Binkley Cheek:
Appalachian Christians Extraordinaire

CONTENTS

FOREWORD
by Mitchell G. Reddish   xi

PREFACE   xv

CHAPTER 1.
Looking for Christian Appalachia
Vanishing Traditions,
Mass Culture, and Lost Mountains

1

CHAPTER 2.
"A Hart Cheareing and Affecting Surmond"
Appalachian Preaching and Preachers

25

CHAPTER 3.
Revisiting the "Woman's Sphere"
Implicit and Explicit Feminism
in Appalachian Churches

47

CHAPTER 4.
Otherness on the Margins
Pentecostal Serpent Handlers
and "No Heller" Primitive Baptists

63

NOTES   83

INDEX   93

FOREWORD

This book derives from a series of lectures, here slightly revised and expanded, delivered at Stetson University in April 2023 by Dr. Bill Leonard. These presentations were the eleventh occurrence (although they constitute only the tenth to be published) of the George H. Shriver Lectures: Religion in American History, a three-part lecture series sponsored by the Department of Religious Studies and the Department of History at Stetson University. The lectures, held at Stetson approximately every other year, were endowed by the late Dr. George Shriver, professor of history emeritus at Georgia Southern University. An alumnus of Stetson University, Dr. Shriver was an author, scholar, and educator who received various awards for his research and teaching.

Dr. Bill Leonard is the founding dean and professor emeritus of the Divinity School at Wake Forest University. After more than twenty years as a professor at the Southern Baptist Theological Seminary and then at Samford University, he took his position at Wake Forest in 1996, serving there until 2010. During that time, he was also professor of church history, professor of religion, and the Dunn Professor of Baptist Studies. He holds the PhD from Boston University. His research focuses on church history with particular attention to American religion, Baptist studies, and religion in Appalachia. A popular speaker and author of around twenty-five books, he has given lectures at a variety of universities including the William James Lecture at Harvard University Divinity School in 2015; the William Self Lectures at McAfee School of Theology, Mercer University, in 2017; and the Whitten Lecture at Baylor University in 2023.

I first became acquainted with Bill Leonard during my initial year as a seminary student when I enrolled in one of Dr. Leonard's church history courses. In the classroom he was witty, insightful, and engaging, as well as a delight to listen to. Since that first class, I have continued to learn from Bill through his writings and his speaking engagements. I can honestly say that I have never been disappointed in one of his presentations and always look forward to hearing what he has to say. One of the best recommendations I can give him is that forty-eight years after that first class with him, I still find him to be witty, insightful, and engaging, as well as a delight to listen to. We had originally planned for him to deliver these lectures in March 2020. However, COVID-19 had other plans. Due to the continuing complications brought about by the pandemic, we had to wait until 2023 to reschedule the lectures. We thought we had everything set for him to deliver the lectures in person on campus, until a few months before the scheduled dates we realized there was a major scheduling conflict. Bill and I worked for weeks to try to find viable alternative dates that worked for both his schedule and Stetson's schedule. When we realized that was not possible, we opted to have him deliver the lectures via Zoom.

The topic of Bill Leonard's lectures was Christianity in Appalachia, a region that has often been studied and frequently misunderstood and misrepresented. Specifically, the lectures focused on certain aspects of local Baptist and Holiness-Pentecostal groups in central Appalachia. Avoiding caricatures of the region and its people, Dr. Leonard provided informed, empathetic assessments of various elements of the religion and culture of Appalachia, including discussions about the beliefs and practices of the groups, the role of preachers, implicit and explicit feminism, Pentecostal snake handling, and "No-Heller" Primitive Baptists.

I express my deepest gratitude to George Shriver for his generosity in establishing this lecture series and also for the presence of him and his wife, Cathy, via Zoom for the 2023 lectures. Unfortunately, a few months after these lectures were delivered, George passed away. One of the ways that his legacy will continue is through this lecture series. I also want to thank Ms. Lisa Guenther, administrative specialist in the Department of Religious Studies at Stetson, for her assistance with the details of these lectures; Dr. Paul Croce, professor of history at Stetson, who serves on the Shriver Lecture Committee with me, for helping to plan and implement the lectures; and the Divinity School at Wake Forest University, and particularly Roger Epps, the school's information technology technician, for assisting with making these virtual lectures work. I would also like to express appreciation to the University of Georgia Press (and especially to Bethany Snead, acquisitions editor) for doing such a great job in publishing the Shriver Lectures ever since the first volume was published in 2003 (full disclosure: I am a UGA alumnus and loyal Dawg fan!).

Mitchell G. Reddish, Chair
George H. Shriver Lectures Committee
Stetson University

PREFACE

It was a great privilege to give the George H. Shriver Lectures for Stetson University in April 2023. Dr. Shriver and I have been friends for decades. We even edited a book together in 1997, the *Encyclopedia of Religious Controversies in the United States*, which brought together a wide variety of scholars. George Shriver's scholarship and classroom teaching remain an outstanding contribution, not only to Georgia Southern University where he spent much of his career, but also to Stetson University, his undergraduate alma mater. I am ever grateful for the friendship that George and Cheryl Shriver have offered me over the years.

That gratitude extends also to Mitchell Reddish and other members of Stetson's Department of Religion with whom I have shared decades of friendship. Their continuing contribution to the lives of their students remains a credit to Stetson University.

APPALACHIAN MOUNTAIN CHRISTIANITY

CHAPTER I

Looking for Christian Appalachia

Vanishing Traditions, Mass Culture,
and Lost Mountains

APPALACHIAN MOUNTAIN CHRISTIANITY:
A UNIQUE ETHOS

Primitive Baptist preachers sometimes weep while they preach, often walking around to shake hands with sinners and look them straight in the eyes; at least the Appalachian ones do it, in white frame meetinghouses, up some hollow, on the edge of time. Howard Dorgan describes the preaching of Elder Wallace Cooper at the Pilgrim Rest Primitive Baptist Church, built over the state lines of Virginia and West Virginia. Dorgan writes that although Cooper is in his eighties, he occasionally, "'Takes the stand,' and when he does the moment becomes a very special one for that PBU [Primitive Baptist Universalist] congregation. Given his advanced age, his preaching is slow and disjointed, but he usually cries when he exhorts, and his emotions inevitably engender a comparable response in his audience." Dorgan notes that unlike most Primitive Baptist men, Cooper's emotions overflow when he gets "happy" in the Spirit.[1] Other mountain Primitive Baptist elders proclaim a more somber gospel, no doubt weighed down by the total depravity that infects all humanity.

Primitive Baptist meetinghouses abound in Appalachia, many used only monthly or quarterly, located off the beaten path where state or county roads may turn to gravel, and near to creeks and

I

CHAPTER ONE

other natural baptismal pools. Natural waters are essential, since outdoor immersion of new believers (average age twenty to thirty) is the norm, and they believe the heated indoor baptisteries of "town churches" undermine the power of that ancient rite. The problem is the Primitives don't trouble the baptismal waters like they used to. Long a minority, their number, like their faith-based culture, is rapidly declining.

Although Primitive Baptists are found throughout the United States, they have long been numbered among the "mountain churches" of the Appalachian region, with their unique approaches to biblical texts, theological dogma, and liturgical practice. The Appalachian Regional Commission defines the Appalachian region as some 206,000 square miles that includes portions of thirteen states from New York to Alabama and all of West Virginia.[2] The focus of this book is on central Appalachia, an area that comprises West Virginia, southwestern Virginia, eastern Kentucky, western North Carolina, and eastern Tennessee, connected to mountainous terrain that includes the Blue Ridge, the Alleghenies, and the Cumberlands.

The Stay Project, a nonprofit organization aimed at "making our [Appalachian] communities where we want and mean to stay," reports that central Appalachia includes 29,773 square miles with a population of almost two million, some 30 percent of which is under age twenty-four. While the region is rife with natural resources, "outside industrial interests have kept the region's people poor." More than 20 percent of residents live below the poverty line, with an income of less than $1,700 a month. The Stay Project's report suggests that central Appalachia "faces challenging problems with education, healthcare, employment and environmental devastation, particularly the economic and social impact of mountaintop removal coal mining."[3]

In her monumental work *Appalachian Mountain Religion: A History* (1995), author Deborah Vansau McCauley notes that one way to investigate Appalachian churches is to focus on a "native mountain church," which "does not belong to national, denominational organizational structures with a national purpose . . . and identity."[4] Her study gives particular attention to the mountain Baptist and independent Holiness churches of the region. Mountain Baptist churches include freestanding individual congregations, associations of like-minded, like-hearted churches, and variously connected, autonomous communions. McCauley identifies them as "subregional organizations" without "national, denominational, organizational structures." Most of these mountain Baptist groups lean toward a Calvinistic approach to the Christian doctrine and practice. Their Reformed theology stands in contrast to the more revivalistic, aggressively conversionist Baptists of the Southern and Independent Baptist variety, the former stressing salvation for a predestined elect and the latter emphasizing the conversion of all who choose to profess faith in Christ.

In *Appalachian Mountain Religion*, McCauley gives extensive evidence to support her contention that "the independent non-denominational church, be it Baptist or Holiness, stands at the center of the spectrum of mountain religious life."[5] She traces the influence of the revival-based nineteenth-century Holiness movement, which had concern for the sanctification of the new believer in the holiness of Christian living through the power of the Holy Spirit. With time, some mountain Holiness churches accepted Pentecostal approaches to sanctification, evidenced in the baptism of the Holy Spirit accompanied by speaking in tongues. McCauley illustrates this process in the evolution of the Church of God (Cleveland, Tennessee) from a coalition of independent mountain churches into an American and global Holiness-Pentecostal denomination.[6]

McCauley also distinguishes "between those church traditions that are in the Appalachian region but not largely of it, mostly the denominations of American Protestantism, and those church tra-

CHAPTER ONE

ditions that exist predominately—or almost exclusively—in the region and are very special to it." Yet she acknowledges that certain denominations, such as United Methodists and Southern Baptists, have a "long history" in Appalachia, with a presence among rural communities, and that these have been "profoundly affected by the distinctive religious culture of the region."[7] McCauley offers a scathing denunciation of the early denominational home-missionary efforts to Christianize the region as if no valid religious communities had previously existed, as well as the later attempts of more liberal "social justice" advocates to "'help' mountain people do battle with more powerful 'oppressors' otherwise out of the reach of their means and skills."[8]

RELIGIOUS EXPERIENCE
IN APPALACHIAN CHURCHES:
THE PARADOX OF "OTHERNESS"

Othering a Culture

This book explores elements of central Appalachian Christianity, with particular attention to certain "mountain" traditions exemplified in Baptist and Holiness-Pentecostal communions and to the "otherness" of their theological and liturgical practices as informed by their varied approaches to personal and communal religious experience. The term "otherness" has been variously applied, dismissively and appreciatively, to issues of both Appalachian society and religion, but it largely refers to the stereotyping of Appalachian people, culture, and faith communities as a marginalized, inferior, or lesser segment of American society.

Mountain Baptist pastor Elder John Sparks warns that "'mainstream' American Protestants" and some academics have often categorized Appalachian religious values "as bizarre, barbaric holdover[s] from days of yore, loud, emotional, fatalistic and superstition-based," with a spectrum that runs from "ultraconservative and traditional Primitive and other 'Old School' Baptists at one extreme or [a] snake-handling minority of the independent Pentecostal subgroups at the other."[9]

In her 2018 book, *Unwhite: Appalachia, Race, and Film*, Meredith McCarroll writes: "Even—and perhaps most especially—from the vantage point of the already othered southerner, Appalachian identity can be seen as a unique form of otherness." Her "work aims to understand the function of the other through a historicized racial lens, specifically interrogating the investment in Appalachia as poor and white." Across the popular culture of the twentieth and twenty-first centuries, she found, "Appalachians were being portrayed using the same lazy methods that had long since been used to portray nonwhites, effectively disempowering [them] through generalized degrading images."[10]

McCarroll contends that the 1974 James Dickey novel *Deliverance*, which became a motion picture in 1976, and the 2016 J. D. Vance memoir *Hillbilly Elegy* illustrate her claim that while the stereotypical Appalachians are genetically white, they have been *othered* by elements of American society that perceive their social place, presence, and behavior as also "unwhite," a regional people cast with a similar sociocultural status as that of Americans of color, who share that imposed otherness. McCarroll concludes: "Appalachia, therefore, exists in the imagination of many passive consumers of these depictions as somewhere between white and nonwhite. The term unwhite . . . evokes this precariously constructed position that at once relies on othering and erases its racial context."[11] A majority of the population is at once racially "pure white stock," yet "in the American imagination at the intersections of race and class," it is nonwhite, "deeply impoverished and backward." For McConnell, the "term *unwhite* draws attention to the simultaneous assumption of and exclusion from an imagined community of whiteness and to the investment in the protection of whiteness."[12]

CHAPTER ONE

Mountain Christianity: The Spirituality of Otherness

Yet otherness is also used to describe particular types of religious experience that focus on encounters with the Divine and contribute to individual and collective spiritual insight. In a study entitled *Emotion, Identity, and Religion: Hope, Reciprocity and Otherness*, Douglas J. Davies acknowledges that "some anthropologists . . . 'reject the very idea of otherness,' believing that it expressed a superiority or imperialism over 'others' as the objects of analysis." Davies's approach, however, posits "otherness" philosophically and existentially "as something inescapable when taking a wide view of ourselves as human beings with emotions and identities and social worlds of our own." Such otherness represents "a certain kind of 'inwardness,' a sense of some inner place where we are able to commune with ourselves—that inner place being one that some believers would also see as a meeting place between one's self and otherness."[13]

In terms of religion, Davies suggests that otherness involves "a constant reminder of the relatedness of persons, whether to others in society, to the environment itself, or to the supernatural influences of which many religions speak." This includes "beliefs and religious doctrines as part of the values of a society," as well as "how sacred texts, rites, and celebrations associated with beliefs become embodied in human feelings, whether in powerful but quickly passing emotions or in influentially enduring moods."[14] The spirituality of the mountain Christian communities highlighted in this book reflects such otherness.

In her widely utilized text *America: Religions and Religion*, historian Catherine Albanese distinguishes between "two kinds of religion," ordinary and extraordinary. Ordinary religion is the source of "cultural forms and the background out of which the norms arise that guide us in our everyday lives." It orients us in discovering "the world as it is and is not," the obvious norms that are taken for granted at the heart of a culture.[15] Extraordinary religion she describes as "an encounter with some form of otherness, whether nat-

6

ural or supernatural." It "gives people names for the unknown and then provides access to a world beyond."[16]

For Albanese, Appalachian mountain churches provide an important illustration of the nature of extraordinary religion. She writes:

> Mountain Christians believed that in the Bible a person would find all that was necessary for salvation and that following the Word of the Bible was literally fundamental. At the same time, religion was understood as feeling deeply felt, and the human experience of conversion was prized as the beginning and end of religious life. Thus, while ordinary religion offered mountain people rules for guidance in everyday situations, Christianity in the mountains held out the desirability of strong feeling as a way to get beyond the ordinary world.[17]

This study acknowledges that Appalachians and their churches have often been "othered" by outsiders, all too easily caricatured, stereotyped, even marginalized in films like *Deliverance* and books like *Hillbilly Elegy*. Yet it also suggests that the spirituality of mountain Christian churches reflects an experiential otherness grounded in the "inwardness" of faith, community, and ritual, much of it rooted in the region's environmental and cultural context. Such spirituality represents a *via media* between the classic spiritual quests for transcendence and imminence—an encounter with the God who is Other, "high and lifted up" (Is 57:15), and with the God who is "Immanuel . . . God with us" (Mt 1:23), incarnate in Jesus of Nazareth.

The beliefs, rituals, and cultural context of mountain churches offer participants, in Douglas Davies' words, "a meeting place between one's self and otherness." In Albanese's words, they offer adherents "names for the unknown," while providing "access to a world beyond." While such spirituality is important in itself and for its participants, it may also inform, if not inspire, a renewed sense of spiritual reflection for those in other Christian contexts. Primitive and Old Regular Baptists, as well as certain Appalachian Holiness-Pentecostal communions, are cases in point.

CHAPTER ONE

PRIMITIVE AND OLD REGULAR BAPTISTS: CALVINISM IN AN APPALACHIAN CONTEXT

Primitive Baptists

This book gives primary attention to the mountain churches, beginning with Primitive and Old Regular Baptists, two denominational illustrations of the depth and uniqueness of Appalachian-based Christian spirituality. The doctrinal features of these churches include:

- *Calvinism.* Primitive and Old Regular Baptists center their biblical interpretations in the theology set forth by John Calvin, the sixteenth-century Protestant reformer of Geneva, Switzerland, with its classic Five Points:

  1. *Total depravity.* Because of the "fall" of Adam and Eve into sin, their offspring, the entire human race, is born into sin, a nature to be removed only by faith in Christ. "[M]an of his own will, without any compulsion and undeceived, transgressed the law of God, falling from his original innocence . . . and involving all his posterity in death in trespasses and sins, in total depravity, in utter inclination to all evil, from which only the saving grace of God can deliver him."[18]

  2. *Unconditional election.* "God, before the foundation of the world, predestined some men to eternal life, through Jesus Christ, . . . and left others to act in their sins to their just condemnation, to the praise of his glorious justice."[19]

  3. *Limited atonement.* "The Father gave all the elect of the human family to the Son in the eternal covenant of grace; the Son, . . . became incarnate of the Virgin Mary, and died and rose again to redeem and justify the elect."[20]

  4. *Irresistible grace.* "The Holy Ghost [or Holy Spirit] regenerates the elect, creating in their souls a new spiritual life,

and effectually applies to them the holy and everlasting salvation of Jesus."[21]

> 5. *Perseverance of the saints.* "[He] infallibly keep[s] every one of them [the elect] unto the fulness of salvation which is to be finally revealed to them."[22]

- *Conversion.* They require conversion of all who will claim membership and baptism into Christ's church, a process initiated and completed only by the Sovereign God who overwhelms with grace the fickle, fallen nature of the human condition.
- *Hope, not assurance, of salvation.* Most say they are "hopefully" saved, since too much assurance is a false security of the believer who has cast everything on Christ for redemption.[23]
- *Suspicion of religious works and training.* Their biblical interpretations lead mountain Primitives to reject Sunday schools, revival meetings, theological seminaries, and missionary endeavors—all "unscriptural" signs of works-righteousness, human efforts to usurp salvific actions that belong to God alone.[24]
- *Unpaid preaching.* Mountain Primitives generally disallow a paid or "hireling" clergy, or preachers specially trained for "the ministry" (as if it were an ordinary, worldly profession). The Black Rock address of 1832 noted: "We decidedly object to persons after professing to have been called of the Lord to preach his gospel, going to a college or academy to fit themselves for that service . . . . [T]he Lord calls no man to preach his gospel, till he has made him experimentally acquainted with that gospel, and endowed him with the proper measure of gifts."[25]
- *Uncertainty.* Scholar Joshua Guthman writes that what made Primitive Baptists distinct from the more revivalistic Baptist and Protestant groups "was their questioning—especially their experience of persistent doubt—that set them apart from their evangelical brethren." The revivalists insisted that salvation was

immediate for those who "called on the name of the Lord" in an experience that involved the sinner's free will to choose Christ and the saving power of God who desired all persons to be saved. The Primitive Baptists believed that salvation came only when God infused salvation into the heart of the elect, enabling them to repent and believe. Guthman insists that they were caught between conversion and doubt: between affirming that God had found them with grace and fearing that they had had fooled themselves regarding the validity of their own salvation. He asserts, "The uncertainty that colored Primitive Baptist selfhood motivated believers rather than paralyzed them. It propelled them toward a community of like-minded souls, and it stirred those souls to action as a more ardent brand of evangelical Protestantism crowded church pews. It is in the Primitives' uncertain selves—not in their theology or in their socio-economic condition—that we find the most compelling explanation of their movement's unlikely rise."[26]

Old Regular Baptists

Primitive Baptist doctrines parallel those of another mountain communion, the Old Regular Baptists, whose Calvinism is modified about half a step. Old Regulars agree with the Primitives that salvation is impossible apart from divine election but insist that such a process does not involve the choice of specific individuals before the foundation of the world. Rather, since grace abounds, all sinners may pursue it, casting themselves on Christ who alone elects individuals to salvation, an "election by grace."[27]

The Primitive and the Old Regular Baptists share many liturgical traditions:

- *The washing of feet.* Along with baptism and the Lord's Supper, they wash feet as a third sacrament, a same-sex washing with men and women divided on either side of the meeting house, "girding themselves" with towels as Jesus did in the John 19 text. "I wouldn't take the bread and the wine," one Old Regular Baptist woman comments, "if I didn't wash feet."[28]

- *Use of wine.* Not all Primitives and Old Regulars bought into the Temperance movement, viewing total abstinence from alcohol as "liberal" and unbiblical, often fermenting their own wine for use in Communion. John G. Crowley cites a Georgia Primitive Baptist who "once remarked that the Missionary [Southern Baptist] and Methodist use of grape juice in Communion was quite appropriate, since their doctrines bore the same resemblance to truth as grape juice bore to wine."[29]
- *A cappella singing.* They eschew musical instruments in church, insisting that "the human voice is the sweetest sound this side of heaven."[30] Their mournful yet hopeful shaped-note plainsong is one of their most familiar Appalachian musical characteristics in the broader American culture.
- *The holy whine.* Mountain Baptist preachers often demonstrate a rhetorical method known as the "holy whine," or "the holy tone," a sing-song chant-like cadence that has sounded across Appalachian Mountains since Baptists first entered the region in the eighteenth century.[31]
- *Biblical authority.* However, mountain Baptists often disagree even among themselves on certain biblical interpretations. In his seminal study *In the Hands of a Happy God: The "No Hellers" of Central Appalachia,* Howard Dorgan describes the practices of the Primitive Baptist Universalists (PBU), a sectarian subgroup of the Primitives numbering no more than about a thousand members in some twenty counties.[32] Pressing their Calvinism to its logical (or illogical) conclusions, the PBUS insist that Christ's atonement is so powerful that it will ultimately save everyone. Everyone experiences varying degrees of punishment right here in this world.[33] That biblical interpretation put the Universalists at odds with those Primitive Baptists who believe that God's grace applies only to the elect,

CHAPTER ONE

chosen for salvation by God alone. The PBUS are detailed later in this text.

MOUNTAIN HOLINESS-PENTECOSTAL CHURCHES

Baptists are not the only mountain Christian communions. Holiness-Pentecostal groups, present from the late nineteenth and early twentieth centuries, expand the theological boundaries of mountain religion with their emphasis on free will and Holy Ghost (or Holy Spirit) baptism—a phenomenon whose fruits are evidenced in glossolalia (speaking in tongues), healing, casting out demons, and (for some) handling serpents and drinking poison. While the terms "Holiness" and "Pentecostal" are often combined to describe certain types of mountain churches, they also define distinct groups that hold parallel views regarding justification, entering into faith, and sanctification, going on in grace.

The Holiness Movement in Appalachia

Taking shape in the latter nineteenth century, the Holiness movement predates Pentecostalism, with an emphasis on a postconversion sanctification through baptism in the Holy Spirit, an ongoing inner spirituality, and outward piety, as emphasized by John Wesley, the founder of Methodism. The Wesleyan Methodist Connection and the Salvation Army, both Holiness-oriented movements, were the first to develop a presence in Appalachia in the late nineteenth century. Other Holiness-related denominations such as the Church of God (originating in Anderson, Indiana) and the Church of the Nazarene would later enter the region.[34]

Late nineteenth-century Holiness revivals set the scene for the founding of the Church of God (Cleveland, Tennessee), an Appalachia-originating Holiness-Pentecostal communion (distinct from the Church of God originating in Anderson, Indiana). The denomination began with the founding of a group that took the name Church of God, coming out of the Christian Union movement founded in Tennessee by Holiness preacher Richard Spurling in 1886. In 1896, a Holiness revival at Camp Creek, North Carolina, took place in which some one hundred participants spoke in tongues (glossolalia). This Appalachian-based Holiness-Pentecostal gathering was organized around speaking in tongues as the "outward and visible sign" of the "inward and spiritual grace" of the baptism of the Holy Spirit. In 1902, the Christian Union was renamed the Holiness Church.

In 1906, a more elaborate organizational structure was approved at a general assembly in Cleveland, Tennessee, and the new denomination constituted as the Church of God. That same year, a revival at the interracial Azusa Street Mission in Los Angeles, California, also led to multiple experiences of glossolalia, events often cited as the beginnings of American Pentecostalism. Church of God historian Donald Bowdle noted, "Thus the roots of Pentecostal belief were planted and nurtured in Appalachian soil, during the Holiness revivals of the latter half of the nineteenth century."[35]

Holiness-Pentecostal Religious Experience

Mountain Holiness-Pentecostal churches give strong emphasis to the experiential elements of Christian faith. Conversion marks the initial entry into relationship with God through Jesus Christ, centered in repentance of sin and profession of faith in Christ. This "new birth" justifies the sinner before God and begins a new life in Christ, outwardly confessed in baptismal immersion. A second stage of Christian faith, the baptism of the Holy Spirit, provides sanctification, a purification of the believer from postbaptismal sin, the outward sign of which is glossolalia, speaking in tongues—a charismatic experience mirroring that of the apostles at Pentecost. This is the first step in the experience of sanctification for holy living. The Declaration of Faith (1948) of the Church of God affirms, "[T]he baptism with the Holy Ghost subsequent to a clean heart" with "speaking with other tongues as the Spirit gives utterance is the initial evidence of the baptism of the Holy Ghost."[36]

CHAPTER ONE

Churchly Order among Holiness-Pentecostals

The Church of God now recognizes three offices for ordained ministers: exhorters, who are called to evangelism, declaring the gospel and urging persons to accept the Christian faith; ministers, who serve as pastors of individual congregations; and bishops, who oversee the administration of the work of the denomination. Females are ordained as exhorters and ministers but are not permitted to serve as bishops.[37]

Mountain Holiness-Pentecostal congregations, sometimes independent and free-standing, sometimes connected to denominations like the Fire-Baptized Holiness Church or the Church of God, demand rigorous ethical responses from all who claim cleansing by the Spirit. Such holiness is evident in dress codes for men and women, abstinence from alcohol and (usually) tobacco, and a general rejection of "worldliness." Those who break the holiness codes are often disciplined, excommunicated, or "churched" in hopes that they may soon repent. Indeed, the emphasis on sanctification is surely one reason that mountain Pentecostals often refer to themselves as simply Holiness in their churchly connections.

The Oneness Pentecostal Movement

Many Pentecostals sometimes divide between trinitarian and "oneness" or "Jesus-only" theology, vehemently disagreeing over whether the post-Pentecost church baptized exclusively in the name of Father, Son, and Holy Ghost or in the name of Jesus only, as many passages of the Book of Acts seem to indicate. I was once at a mountain Holiness serpent-handling revival where the trinitarian preacher articulated these divisions with perfect homiletical clarity: "Jesus had a Daddy," he declared. "He wasn't no bastard."

As early as 1913, certain Pentecostal preachers determined that the Book of Acts taught baptism in the name of Jesus only—"Repent and be baptized every one of you in the name of Jesus

Christ" (Acts 2:38)—rather than the trinitarian formula, "baptizing them in the name of the Father and of the Son and of the Holy Spirit" (Mt 28:19). Frank Ewart, one of the early leaders of Oneness Pentecostalism, concluded: "We saw that if the name of the Father, Son, and Holy Spirit was Jesus Christ, then in some mysterious way, the Father, Son, and Holy Ghost were made one in the person of Jesus Christ. We saw from this premise that the old trinity debate was unscriptural."[38] Thus, Oneness Pentecostals assert that to baptize in the name of Jesus alone is to incorporate the whole trinitarian formula.

DENOMINATIONAL CHURCHES
IN CENTRAL APPALACHIA

Denominational rural and "town" churches—Missionary, Free Will, and Independent Baptists, Free Methodists, Nazarenes, and other evangelical groups—also thrive in Appalachia, many holding tenaciously to a fundamentalist conservatism that parallels the mountain sects, as reflected in their conversionism, their opposition to worldliness, their commitment to classic fundamentals of Protestant faith—inerrant Bible, Christ's virgin birth and substitutionary atonement, his bodily resurrection and premillennial second coming.

Many denominationally based churches continue to conduct seasonal revivals, mourn the decline of hellfire preaching, and send out missionaries locally, regionally, and globally. Some call pastors trained at seminaries or Bible schools, maintain staffed ministries, and struggle to adapt themselves to a changing culture where older evangelistic methods no longer seem to captivate souls as they once did. Others—United Methodists, Episcopalians, Lutherans, Presbyterians, and progressive Baptists of various stripes—are mainline ecumenical in their approach to ministry, liturgy, and theology, many now calling ordained women as senior or associate pastors. The term mainline, first applied during the fundamentalist-

CHAPTER ONE

modernist debates of the 1920s, was used to describe those groups ensconced at the center of American Protestant life and cultural influence. Later on, they were referenced as the ecumenical denominations.

MOUNTAIN CHURCHES IN THE TWENTY-FIRST CENTURY: THE CHALLENGES

Any discussion of the radical transition now underway in Appalachian religion must begin by acknowledging the distinct religious traditions with historic roots in the region. Deborah McCauley asserts that "mountain religion" should not be confused with "southern religion," or viewed as a mere subgroup of majority denominational traditions. Nor is it to be caricatured as the "religion of the poor," an approach that McCauley calls "pernicious, insidious, and condescending." Rather, it is a unique form of Protestantism born of "oral tradition," the "centrality of religious experience," and the "reality of the *land*."[39] Indeed, McCauley concludes that "the mountainous terrain that is the Appalachian region has had enormous impact on its character, its texture, and its religious values."[40] Thirty years after the publication of her much-cited study, the forms of mountain religion she traced are fast declining, hard-hit by demographic shifts, the rise of mass culture, and the destruction of the very mountains that gave religion its identity. Mainline denominational churches are not far behind, feeling their Protestant privilege challenged in the public square by a new religious pluralism now evident even in rural Appalachia.

Such losses are recognized by many of the practitioners themselves. In fact, some have long viewed changes in mountain culture as having apocalyptic implications. In *Foxfire 7*, part of a multivolume series of student-gathered oral histories from Appalachia, published in 1982, Primitive Baptist Howard Parham warned,

> The biggest sign [that the end is near] to me is how progress has been made in the last seventy-five years. . . . After World War II everything,

approximately, is push-button. . . . [Progress] is the biggest sign that things are getting near the end. It's rolling faster and faster—like a ball going down a hill. . . . So the end is coming on. In my day, just in my day, the world has changed. According to the scripture, we're in the last evening now. That's the way I believe, and I've heard a lot of Primitive Baptists say it. We're in the evening of time. I do believe that.[41]

Today, Elder Parham would no doubt admit that time rolls on, Jesus tarries, and Primitive Baptists, at least in Appalachia, are declining while secular worldliness continues unabated. Mass culture, in its varied expressions, has overtaken Appalachia as never before, a phenomenon particularly evident in religious life. Appalachia has long served as a case study for examining transitions in the larger American culture.

The twenty-first century brought numerous challenges to Appalachia as significant elements of American mass culture inched their way throughout the region, dramatically impacting a once unique segment of the country. Religious idiosyncrasies should not be dismissed as romanticized sentimentalism but as a reflection of significant theological, liturgical, and cultural distinctiveness. Even the briefest survey illustrates the extent of the change that is affecting churches throughout the region.

- *Ecclesiology.* Appalachia is not immune from the "megachurching" of America, an ecclesiastical phenomenon occurring from coast to coast. Megachurches are found throughout Appalachia, many doing for Appalachian ecclesiology what Walmart has done for sales and services, positioning themselves on the edges of towns or counties, drivable from throughout the region, often growing in direct proportion to the decline of mom-and-pop churches in the area. Most megachurches offer "Bible preaching," conservative doctrine, and spirited, charismatic—if not Pentecostal—worship that parallels traditional mountain congregations. Yet they provide "full service" programs for varied age groups, multiple choices for ministry action, and media-savvy technology, all located

CHAPTER ONE

within easy driving distance, especially for young singles and families. Though a single congregation, they are essentially mini-denominations, offering the services and ministries previously provided by larger denominations—mission, education, publication, evangelism, and identity.

- *Technology.* If you drive across central Appalachia, what sign of technology is most obvious outside many roadside houses? A satellite dish, a tool of connection to global mass culture—multichanneled, with satellite sources like Viasat Internet. Consider all the "worldliness" that such technology brings into the region, much as it does to global culture. Mountain preachers might be concerned about that, except many are also online. Yet as satellite dishes bring "worldliness," they also bring virtual religion, 24-7 Christian broadcasting, linking mountain believers with all sorts of religious ideas, methods, worship styles, and ideologies—most of them distinctly conservative, but nonetheless diverse. Think of all the diversity satellite TV brings into Appalachia: T. D. Jakes and Creflo Dollar in Black megachurches; the Gaither family with their old-style new-age gospel music; EWTN network broadcasting Catholicism 24-7; Joel and Victoria Osteen insisting that God feels good about himself and you should too; the Mormon Tabernacle Choir broadcast "from beneath the shadow of the everlasting hills"; and assorted online streams of regional churches large and small. Perhaps no single force is impacting Appalachian church life, worship, and Christian identity like the technology of televised, online religion.
- *Music.* Hymnody and other musical forms illustrate the impact of mass religious culture in the region, drawn from both megachurch practices and the diversity brought by technology. Old forms still remain, but there are new options, including praise choruses, old gospel, and what some call "Jesus is my boyfriend" worship songs. The use of recorded music has come to many church choirs and singing groups

18

in the region in ways that extend or challenge prevailing musical traditions. Yet through it all, the a cappella shaped-note voices of the Primitive and Old Regular Baptists continue to sound across the hollows.

BOOK BURNING IN NORTH CAROLINA: THE CHANGING CULTURAL LANDSCAPE

One extreme but telling response to this theological pluralism was evident in 2009 when the Amazing Grace Baptist Church in Canton, North Carolina, staged its first annual "book burning" to roast translations of the Bible including the RSV, NRSV, and NIV. The plan was also to burn books by Billy and Franklin Graham, Mark Driscoll, Robert Schuller, Rick Warren, John MacArthur, Charles Colson, and other notable evangelicals—as well as the pope, for good measure. They also proposed to burn CDs of both secular and contemporary Christian music. The church's web page invited believers to attend, concluding with the note that "we are serving fried chicken and all the sides." A local sheriff reminded the pastor that book burning is illegal in North Carolina, so the incident was more symbolic than smoky.

Nonetheless, it is clear that some mountain churches see their theology compromised by secularists and evangelicals alike,[42] thanks to the morphing spiritual, social, and natural landscapes.

- *Globalism.* Globalism has come to Appalachia, evident in the development of new religious communities and the small but increasing presence of non-Christian religions. CBS News' *Eye on America* once called Asheville, North Carolina, "America's New Age Mecca," highlighting the "mystical" sensations that vibrate around the Blue Ridge Mountain town.[43] Such religious globalism is hard to miss. There is a storefront Islamic Society in downtown Asheville, North Carolina, and an Eckankar meditation center down the street. Namaste Yoga at 75a Cumberland Avenue is one of some fifteen to twenty such

CHAPTER ONE

establishments throughout the city. Wiccans remain a controversial but public presence in Asheville as well. In October 1999, Leni Sitnick, the mayor of Asheville, North Carolina, decided to declare "Earth Religions Awareness Week" in that Protestant-infested mountain city. Irate evangelical clergy demanded that the mayor declare the next week "Lordship of Jesus Christ Week." She refused and, the story goes, gave up the religious week business altogether.[44] Globalism makes slow but steady inroads in the mountains.

- *Demography.* Demographic realities are at the heart of transitions in Appalachian religious traditions and the impact of mass culture. Declining birth rates in mountain families have a direct bearing on the perpetuation of traditional faith. In an earlier era, large mountain families sustained farming, provided a ready labor force, and offered social security to generations. They also established a constituency for passing on religious identity. Primitive Baptists rejected direct evangelism but reproduced themselves biologically in sufficient numbers to keep their movement sustained. Likewise, the term "stem family churches" is used to describe congregations involving a group of families, related not only by faith perspectives, but also by a high degree of kinship through intermarriage. Nonetheless, declining birthrates and increasing mobility have taken their toll on the Primitives and the Old Regulars as young people leave the region or attend town churches with multiple youth programs. In a sense, biology again sustains theology.
- *Environment.* The most dramatic symbol of the loss of Appalachian regional and religious identity is in the environment. Clear and present danger has reached crisis proportions as forests disappear, condominiums clutter hillsides and claim woodlands, streams and creeks are crammed with sludge, and mining continues to make the landscape bleak. But in twenty-first-century Appalachia, the most sobering reality is the loss of the mountains themselves. Through coal-mining

mountaintop removal techniques, mountains formed over five million years ago have vanished from the face of the earth, their noncoal contents tossed into valleys, creek beds, and hollows, with devastating effects. Appalachian studies professor Ron Eller writes that "with few exceptions" the promised economic benefits of mountaintop removal "never materialized, and communities were left with miles of deserted, treeless plateaus, poisoned water tables, and a permanently altered landscape."[45] If Deborah McCauley is correct that Appalachian religious experience was shaped in part by the "reality of the *land*," then the culture and religion of Appalachia may be vanishing with the vanishing mountains. Zeb Mountain, Turner Spur, Peters Knob, Big Fork Ridge, Millard, Cow Knob, Cherry Pond, and Payne Knob are but a few names of the over five hundred mountains from Kentucky, West Virginia, and Virginia that have disappeared from the face of the earth, never to return.[46] Psalm 121 in the KJV begins, "I lift up mine eyes unto the hills." Not anymore, in certain segments of Appalachia. So how will mountain Christians sing the Lord's song in a foreign land?

MOUNTAIN CHURCHES: NURTURING FAITH, CONFRONTING CULTURE

Historic religious traditions long present in Appalachia are declining or vanishing with the mountains. Some needed to go, no doubt since bigotry, racism, sexism, and cruelty in God's name require repentance wherever such attitudes and actions exist. Appalachian Protestants berate each other over which Bible to read and what to drink at Communion or at dinner. Their churches split readily over everything from fundamental doctrines to the seemingly mundane: from the doctrine of the Trinity, women preachers, and whether to pay the pastor or what color to paint the meetinghouse. They live hard, get saved hard, and fall off the grace wagon hard. But as large

CHAPTER ONE

pieces of their religious culture disappear or are absorbed by mass religious identities, there are some lessons that should not be lost on all American Christians.

First, mountain churches reflect quite tangibly the strength and danger of sacraments and symbols. Sacraments are the enacted word of God, the word of God without words. They help Christians get their bearings in the world, a means of grace in a land where all kinds of claims are made in the name of God and where American evangelicalism has been politicized perhaps beyond repair. The sacraments of baptism, Holy Communion, and foot washing link Christians of every generation with their origins, a continuity of historic otherness. They are reminders of new birth, life, death, and care for others. Their spiritual otherness remains an outward and visible sign of an inward and spiritual grace.

Second, mountain churches demonstrate the power of oral tradition and strength of story that nurture the spirituality of both transcendence and immanence—the God who is sovereign and separate and the God who is "Immanuel . . . God with us" (Mt 1:23). They give evidence to the power of the spoken and proclaimed word to cultivate religious experience, pass on identity, and renew the meaning of the Jesus Story in every generation.

Yet oral tradition is not limited to preaching. It is inseparable from the life and witness of the religious community itself. Deborah McCauley writes that "this informal—indeed, spontaneous— quality is the creative aspect of traditional religion."[47] Appalachian oral tradition calls us to take seriously the rhetoric of spontaneity and vulnerability and its capacity to re-form the gospel before our very eyes and ears.

Finally, Appalachian religious communities embody the value and fragility of sacred space, the struggle to maintain it, and the identity crisis that inevitably results when it slips away. In doing so, many have discovered the grace of dissent.

In a 2007 sermon at Cherry Log Christian Church in Cherry

Log, Georgia, Appalachian scholar and social activist Helen Lewis declared that Jesus "developed alternative ways of meeting the needs of the people. His ministry was an alternative to the established, inadequate ways of dealing with health problems. He developed what I would describe as shade tree clinics, and alternative ways of dealing with the poor and hungry by sharing food in the countryside."[48]

Lewis recalled the work of Eula Hall in Mud Creek, Kentucky, "who developed an alternative health clinic because the health needs were not being met in Mud Creek." She referenced "the 61-year old Widow [Ollie] Combs who sat down in front of a bulldozer in Kentucky and was carried off the strip mine site and spent Thanksgiving Day in jail for obstructing the mining operation on her land."[49] Lewis concluded: "Our goal is a new creation, transformation, the reign of God, the beloved community, and we need a clear vision of what that can be."[50]

Appalachian Christians learned faith up hollows, on mountainsides, by cold, clear streams, and in deep lush valleys. They spent decades renegotiating that faith with strip mines and strip malls, slag pits and condominium complexes, polluted rivers and manhandled mountains. They confront a world often moving as fast as it can to undo sacred space across the globe.

When the creature, not the Creator, "make[s] waste mountains and hills and dr[ies] up all their herbs," when the creature, not the Creator, "make[s] the rivers islands and . . . dr[ies] up the pools" (Is 42:15, KJV); when the creature, not the Creator, makes the crooked straight and the rough places plain, then maybe Jesus should hurry back and straighten all this out.

But if Jesus continues to tarry, the mountains continue to vanish, and the church on earth remains, then we had best engage in serious gospel action on behalf of God's good creation, else we will be forced to learn to sing the Lord's song in a treeless, mountainless land.

CHAPTER 2

"A Hart Cheareing and Affecting Surmond"

Appalachian Preaching and Preachers

THE STUDY OF PREACHING IN APPALACHIA

In his study of *Primitive Baptists in the Wiregrass South*, John G. Crowley describes the early presence of the Primitive Baptists in the Appalachian region, specifically at Union Church, Lakeland, Georgia, whose 1854 meeting house still stands.[1] He highlights something of the worship and preaching at this church, where services were held monthly on the second Saturday and Sunday and included "singing, prayer, and preaching by whatever Baptist ministers, if any, were present."[2] Crowley documents one specific sermon preached by the Reverend Matthew Albritton on Sunday, August 9, 1829, as transcribed by another preacher, William Knight. The text was Mark 15:16—"And the soldiers led him away into the hall, called Praetorium; and they called together the whole band"—not a highly familiar text even then. In his notes on the sermon, Knight comments that Brother Albritton "was in the fullness of the gospel and by inspiration delivered to us a hart cheareing and affecting Surmond [Sermon]" so powerful that "a goodly number gave him there [sic] hand to be praid [sic] for."[3]

APPALACHIA:
THE CONTEXT FOR PREACHING

The phrase "a heart-cheering and affecting sermon" came to mind when the Stetson University religion department chair, Mitchell

CHAPTER TWO

Reddish, asked me to focus the 2023 Shriver Lectures on certain religious traditions and practices present in the central Appalachian region. No such study is complete, I think, without a consideration of Appalachian preaching. This may seem a moot point since every year fewer Americans listen to sermons regularly, if at all. Nonetheless, the lessons of Appalachian preaching and preachers in this particular context remain informative both inside and outside American churches.

Questions abound. Can Appalachian theological and homiletical forms and formulas, at once so intense, so contextual, and often so ecclesiastically distinctive, have any real application for a pluralistic society increasingly dominated by social media, climate change, and religious nonaffiliation? Do rhetorical and doctrinal modes born of revivalism, conversionism, pietism, and mountain spirituality offer insights for a church culture often divided into assorted homiletical camps shaped by "worship wars," "culture wars," Christian nationalism, and other sociotheological divisions?

And what of Appalachia itself? As strip malls dot a landscape increasingly "brought low" by mountaintop removal and condominium construction, are its once self-evident regional cultural and religious "markers" simply vanishing? Appalachian churches may be no more intact than congregations in the rest of postmodern America.

Let us not lose heart. In fact, if heart-cheering and affecting sermons remain essential to the church's homiletical task, then might certain Appalachian preaching practices provide important motifs for addressing, even challenging, the contemporary Protestant pulpit, offering options for renewing authentic religious experience?

At the same time, such preaching may be less a model for current pulpiteers than an illustration of the way in which preachers in one historical setting responded to timeless issues of theology, pastoral care, worship, and textual exegesis confronted by preachers in every era. While the homiletical and theological underpinnings of many Appalachian preachers are often distinct from, even at odds with, the larger church, their ways of responding to the challenges and dilemmas encountered in the church and in the world, in the dogmas and the biblical texts, amid human frailty and blatant sinfulness, may help us confront our own spiritual and cultural quandaries here and now.

To consider these preachers and their homiletical mystique is to confess that some things may not transfer easily if at all; theological and hermeneutical approaches, as well as doctrinal and ethical disagreements, abound in the mountains and beyond. Cultural location compels ministry in unique ways that do not necessarily compute or combine. We enter the region and the subject cautiously and respectfully, recognizing that Appalachian churches and the culture they inhabit confront their own religiosocial upheavals.

APPALACHIAN CHURCHES IN A TIME OF PERMANENT TRANSITION

Appalachian churches are not immune from an era of permanent transition that impacts congregations and denominations across America. Demographics reflect transitions in rural Appalachian churches as well in urban faith communities. Declining birth rates and multigenerational departures mean that many of the traditional mountain churches face uncertain futures. The changing sociology of Sunday means that even churchgoing families may be forced to attend less than in previous years since Sunday now carries continued demands of work, family responsibilities, recreation, and other stresses. Likewise, disengagement from religious communities by "nones," those who claim no religious affiliation, is as real in Appalachian mountain and rural churches as it is in the rest of America.[4]

Congregations, even traditional ones, are also in transition. Students in Wake Forest School of Divinity's annual Appalachian religion course discovered that reality between 2010 and 2020. On

CHAPTER TWO

one occasion, the class visited what they believed to be a "traditional" mountain church in Bat Cave, North Carolina, only to discover that the pastor utilized PowerPoint outlines to highlight his sermons, that the church had deserted its older meeting house for a new multipurpose facility, and that traditional gospel hymnody had been replaced by praise choruses, music one critic described as "one note, two words, three hours!" A Wesley Theological Seminary student opined: "I could have stayed in D.C. and watched Joel Osteen on TV!" That Sunday the class experienced yet another challenge to Appalachian religious stereotypes. Modernity had found its way into a traditional mountain congregation.

Given this rapidly developing reality, what might we learn from Appalachian preaching that could sharpen our own responses to similar religious transitions nationwide? How can mountain preachers possibly teach anything that postmodern sinners might find spiritually beneficial? In *Plurality and Ambiguity: Hermeneutics, Religion, and Hope* (1987), University of Chicago theologian David Tracy explores the essence of hermeneutics (interpretation)in broad ways that might inform our own efforts to explore the nature and impact of Appalachian preaching. He writes,

> Interpretation seems a minor matter, but it is not. Every time we act, deliberate, judge, understand, or even experience, we are interpreting. To understand at all is to interpret. . . . We admittedly cannot offer a fully explicit account of the complex human skill of interpreting any more than we could offer such an account of any one of our other practical skills. Nevertheless, studying a variety of models for understanding this central but puzzling phenomenon can aid us in developing the practices necessary for good interpreters: those that enrich our experience, allow for understanding, aid deliberation and judgment, and increase the possibilities of meaningful action.[5]

Tracy concludes that "anyone can also learn interpretation theories (or hermeneutics). Then we may use these theories as they should be used: as further practical skills for the central task of becoming human."[6] What are some interpretive elements of Appalachian preaching that might help preachers and their listeners, in the mountains and beyond, to discover spiritual insights for becoming more human?

Any study of Appalachian preaching must walk that thin line of celebrating the significant indigenous forms found in pulpits in various communions while avoiding the danger of caricatures. In *Appalachian Mountain Religion*, Deborah McCauley warned of those perils, writing that "mountain preachers suffer the fate of being portrayed either as drab, oppressive, narrow purveyors of doctrinal darkness (read 'Calvinism') or as emotional exotics left over from the worst excesses of the Great Revival." Such caricature, she notes, "obliterates mountain religion's broad spectrum of worship practices, belief systems, church traditions, and religious culture."[7]

McCauley's comments lead us to acknowledge that before we ask what aspects of mountain preaching and preachers might inform our own ideas and religiocultural responses, we need to reflect on the nature of that preaching as distinct in and of itself.

MOUNTAIN PREACHERS: FROM CALL TO CONTENT

A brief survey of identifiable marks of those preaching traditions sets the scene for discussion of their homiletical and liturgical insights.

First, mountain preachers begin with the call to preach, a powerful entry point in mountain churches across the denominational spectrum. The call is a postconversion spiritual experience that provides divine empowerment for the preacher's task, a clear sign of spiritual otherness rooted in the call of prophets and apostles in both testaments, undergirding the preacher's sense of mission. *Foxfire 7* (1982) includes interviews with mountain preachers who give accounts of their callings. Charles Lee, a preacher in the Fire-Baptized Holiness Church, recalls, "When the Lord called me to preach, it seemed like the Bible came before me and the pages were being turned like something coming off a press. Just like a newspaper coming off a press. I saw later on that when I was preaching the pages of the Bible would be on my mind and they turned like [that] because I preach fast. I can't preach no other way except fast. . . . When I get to preaching, why, it just comes to me."[8] Baptist preacher Clyde Nations Jr. told his student interviewer: "God was personally calling me. I was anointed, and when I use the word 'anointed,' I speak of the power of God. There was many hours I laid awake. I could vision myself preaching to congregations of people. I visioned people being saved under my preaching and this is how I felt God dealing with me."[9] The sense of call sustains these preachers in the tough times they confront in the church and the world at large. For Appalachian Christians, the call gives divine credentials to those who claim the ministry of the Word in the church.

Second, mountain preachers preach for conversion. They are, to use one of William James's categories of religious experience, "twice-born" in their understanding of how one encounters the grace of God. James wrote that "in the religion of the twice-born . . . the world is a double-storied mystery. . . . There are two lives, the natural and the spiritual, and we must lose the one before we can participate in the other."[10]

James defines conversion in his classic *Varieties of Religious Experience* (1902):

> To be converted, to be regenerated, to receive grace, to experience religion, to gain an assurance, are so many phrases which denote the process, gradual or sudden, by which a self hitherto divided and consciously . . . unhappy, becomes unified and consciously . . . happy, in consequence of its firmer hold upon religious realities. This at least is what conversion signifies in general terms, whether or not we believe that a direct divine operation is needed to bring such a moral change about.[11]

Appalachia remains a region in which James's definition of conversion becomes incarnate. In 2015, students in the Wake Forest course on Appalachian religion heard the "conversion testimony" of a twentysomething Yancey County male who recounted a life of youthful "riotous" living—cooking meth, drinking hard, and driving fast—all brought to a cathartic end by a horrific pickup crash in which he and his friends were all spared from what should have been certain death. Realizing the grace of that terrible moment, Adam "received Christ as his personal Savior," much to the delight of his Free Will Baptist mother, who, he recalled, shouted praises to Jesus for days after. Adam preaches frequently at the county jail, where he knows he would have wound up but for the fact that none of his friends died in the pickup he was driving and the judge, like Jesus, gave him a second chance. His story was so powerful, one of the seminarians observed that "even the Presbyterian students" were reduced to tears.[12]

Personal conversion is a central tenet of mountain preachers, some calling sinners to immediate repentance and faith at the close of the sermon, others, with more Calvinist orientation, urging the unconverted to "wait on the Lord" who alone is the agent of salvation. In many congregations, the preacher issues an "altar call," inviting the "unsaved" to "walk the aisle" of the church to receive Christ as Savior and Lord. Preachers must be well acquainted with the "plan of salvation," necessary for guiding sinners through repentance, faith, and prayers that reflect a conscious decision to "invite Jesus into your heart" and to profess newfound faith in him. At the same time, mountain preachers are also required to "admonish the saved," those who claim conversion but sometimes backslide or "fall off the grace wagon," urging them to practice Christianity in their daily lives.

Third, mountain preachers are restorationists, convinced that they must mirror the New Testament church in faith and practice, while differing in their specific denominational communities regarding what New Testament principles and practices to restore. Many of the Baptists believe that they have little to reinstate, since their tradition alone has preserved "primitive" gospel practices unbroken since Jesus's baptism by John (the Baptist!) in the River Jordan. Holiness folks insist that the Pentecostal power, squandered by Catholic and Protestant traditions alike, was lost or minimized until recovered by Pentecostals in the early twentieth century. Thus the Pentecostal gifts of tongues, healing, and Spirit possession are unmistakable evidence that the Holy Spirit has been poured out anew as a sign of the "latter rain" in preparation for the return of Jesus.

Fourth, mountain preachers assert an abiding biblicism, often summarized by the affirmation: "The Bible says it, I believe it, and that settles it." But biblical authority and biblical hermeneutics often don't lead to the same theological conclusions. Diverse communions may insist on the inerrant authority of Scripture while vehemently disagreeing on what the authoritative text means and requires.

Pentecostal hermeneutics links the Bible and the Spirit inseparably with the assertion that the same Holy Spirit that fell on the apostles at Pentecost is the Holy Spirit that enlivens the hearts and minds of latter day Appalachian Pentecostals. Like their biblical, post-Pentecost spiritual ancestors, they speak in tongues, offer and receive physical and spiritual healing, cast out demons, and proclaim the gospel in word and deed. For them, the Spirit is the source of justification and sanctification as taught in Scripture and exemplified in the beliefs and actions of the Spirit-led church. Water baptism is the outward sign of justification by faith in Christ, while glossolalia is the outward sign of the Holy Spirit's descent into the heart of the justified, born-again individual, providing the power to live the "sanctified life" of Christian sanctification.

Fifth, there is Appalachian culture. Time rolls on, Jesus tarries, and many mountain Baptist and Pentecostal congregations are in decline. In fact, change is so pervasive in the Appalachian region that scholars and citizens both urban and rural acknowledge what one observer told divinity school students.

Mass culture, in its varied expressions, has taken its toll on

Appalachia as never before, a phenomenon particularly evident in religious life. Perhaps American Christianity itself is perched on the edge of what Robert Orsi calls another religious "remaking" when he writes: "Americans have been compelled to make and re-make their worlds and themselves endlessly, relentlessly, on constantly shifting grounds, in often brutal economic circumstances, and religion has been one of [the]—if not *the*—primary media through which this work of making and remaking has proceeded."[13]

In many ways, Appalachian religion and culture have always been in transition. Whether in strip mining or Holy Ghost baptism, Appalachian Christians were impacted by economic realities and new movements that continually descended on traditional communities. What insights might Christians inside and outside the region learn from Appalachian preaching and preaching cultures?

MOUNTAIN PREACHERS
AND HOMILETICAL IDENTITY

How do Appalachian mountain preachers understand their own homiletical identity in the context of specific congregations and belief systems? Deborah McCauley calls mountain preaching a tradition "that relies exclusively on what is experienced and perceived to be the direct inspiration of the Holy Ghost." She compares mountain preachers with Protestantism's "dominant religious culture . . . which places its highest premium on a learned clergy and their self-control, their self-consciousness and deliberative intentionality in the pulpit." By contrast, McCauley suggests that "in the mountain churches, God speaks *through* the preacher who does everything in his (or her) power to step aside, simply to be 'a willing instrument' and not get too much in the way." This, she believes, leads many Appalachian preachers to nurture and experience "humbleness," a spiritual attempt to "fade . . . into the background" giving maximum space to the Spirit.[14]

CHAPTER TWO

Whatever else may be said about mountain preachers, it is surely clear that they let you know when they are coming. They have discovered a rhetorical framework for their response to the gospel in ways that captivate their hearers, drawing them to faith, repentance, or antagonism. In his study *The Roots of Appalachian Christianity*, United Baptist Elder John Sparks describes the earliest rhetorical tradition of the eighteenth-century revivalistic Separate Baptists, whose pulpit styles set a pattern of Appalachian preaching, and traces it back to Shubal Stearns and Daniel Marshall, founders of the Sandy Creek Baptist Church in North Carolina in the 1750s. Sparks cites the eighteenth-century Baptist historian Morgan Edwards's comments on Stearns's distinctive rhetoric. Edwards wrote: "Mr. Stearns was but a little man, but of good natural parts, and sound judgement. Of learning he had but a small share, yet was pretty well acquainted with books. His voice was musical and strong, which he managed in such a manner, as one while to make soft impressions on the heart, and fetch tears from the eyes in a mechanical way; and anon to shake the nerves, and to throw the animal system into tumults and perturbations."[15] Edwards concluded that "all the Separate ministers copy him in terms of voice and actions of body; and some few exceed him. His character is indisputably good both as a man, a Christian, and a preacher."[16] Might twenty-first-century preachers be able to offer sermons that "throw the animal system into tumults," let alone "perturbations"?

Edwards noted that congregational "outcries, epilepsies and exstasies [sic]" were not limited to Stearns and the Baptists but were also evident among Yankee Presbyterians in North Carolina and revivalistic Anglicans in Virginia. He observed that "the enchantments of sounds, attended with corresponding actions," might not be unique to Baptists, yet they seemed providentially evident in the Separate Baptist communities through an "invisible hand . . . bearing down the human mind, as was the case in primitive churches."[17]

For most Appalachian preachers then and now, sermon prepa-

34

ration began with prayer and Bible study, but the delivery depended on the immediate involvement of the Holy Ghost. In her 1905 book *The Spirit of the Mountains*, Emma Bell Miles described a worship service led by Brother Absalom Darney, writing, "Like other mountain preachers, he speaks readily on his feet without preparation, scarcely once opening a book of which he can repeat whole pages by heart."[18]

Speech professor Howard Dorgan noted that most mountain preachers "never prepare sermons" in a formal sense, but "instead they 'take the stand' and deliver wholly improvised messages, believing that written or outlined sermons" reflect human attempts at rhetorical content that should come from divine inspiration alone. Dorgan observed that sermons often reflect "a rhythmical delivery pattern that has become the hallmark of Appalachian preaching—a chanted, sung, or wailed vocal style, dominated by a pronounced cadence and accompanied by an equally dynamic set of physical behaviors."[19] This phrasing and breathing cadence is sometimes known as the "holy whine" or the "holy tone," since it is most closely associated with preaching and preachers.

These breathing techniques seem inseparable from the spontaneity of the sermon content, allowing the preacher to signal that the format has moved from a churchly "talk" to a word from the Divine. The breathing pauses also permit the preacher to give brief but significant space to decide what to say next. Dorgan agreed, noting that this traditional sermonic "delivery mode" permits speakers "to manage the exuberance and speed of their sermons by providing a systematic breathing pattern, a functional way to regulate air intakes while exhorting at delivery rates that may approach or exceed two hundred words per minute."[20]

Dorgan also commented that the preachers seldom "begin their sermons by immediately falling into these fast-paced, energetic, soaring styles." Rather, they often commence rather awkwardly, struggling somewhere between flesh and spirit, waiting, and hoping to "pull a message down from heaven." The waiting congregation receives the word in the classic "call and response," urging preachers to relinquish "self" to Spirit and go on from there.

Ultimately, the preacher "quickens" the homiletical pace, moving toward a "choppy and punchy cadence," often with a gesture that takes the "right hand up to a spot just behind or below" the ear, a sign that the sermon has begun and the messenger given way to the Spirit.[21] Preachers may address listeners by name or move among them shaking hands, but as Dorgan comments, they often seem "captivated by [their] own spell, engaged in a form of visual and audio dynamics . . . largely oblivious to external distractions."[22]

This approach is evident in many descriptions of Appalachian proclaimers and the power of their rhetoric. Berea College folklorist Loyal Jones recounts Alabama Methodist John Lakin Brasher's account of his ministerial mentor, the antislavery preacher T. R. Parker, who made a post–Civil War visit to an Alabama church where his opponents had drawn a skull and crossbones on the door, warning him to stay away. Undeterred, Parker began to preach. Brasher recalled that before his mentor "got through, some of those fellows that'd come to murder him leaped up and grabbed him around the neck and hugged him, and they celebrated together. He'd swept them off their feet."[23]

Brasher said this about Parker's preaching:

> When he began to soar in his eloquence, he seemed to forget the audience was present, and taking a sort of look slantingly upward, puckering up his fingers as if he were hold of a thread, he began to climb, and climb, and climb—with a great marvelous [crescendo]. Sometimes he would get up and say, "I do not feel very much like preaching this morning. I will give you a little talk." And then he'd start unfolding the Scriptures, and the first thing you know, he was preaching one of the greatest sermons that [anybody] ever listened to.[24]

Brasher's accounts are powerful sermonic commentaries of their own: "soar in his eloquence"; "climb, and climb, and climb"; "unfolding the Scriptures." Wonderful images of the homiletical art.

In their study of the Primitive Baptists, James Peacock and Ruel Tyson Jr. delineated three types of sermons used in many Appalachian churches as understood to be "authorized by scripture." These include (1) "doctrinal" preaching, which addresses basic theological and confessional issues that are central to the faith; (2)"experimental" preaching, which "focuses on the spiritual experience of biblical characters, usually coupled with similar experiences" in the lives of the preachers and those who know them; and (3) "duty preaching," which puts emphasis on the responsibilities of believers to fulfill their Christian calling, particularly to the church.[25] Many churches differentiate between a sermon and an exhortation, the latter a call to Christian discipleship and religious experience and the former aimed at articulating Christian doctrine, often moving in a decidedly Calvinist direction on issues of God's sovereignty, judgment, and mercy.

There are dangers, of course. Sometimes the prophetic becomes petty, attacking demons long since exorcized or spiritual enemies long since vanquished. Sometimes the call for church discipline of recalcitrant sinners becomes a diatribe that drives away as many as repent. Sometimes guilt and shame prevail, even for those who are born again. Battle lines over dogma divide churches and families across the years and the landscape. We dare not romanticize.

Whatever the form of the sermon, many Appalachian preachers articulate a constant "spiritual warfare" between self and Spirit in the sermonic event. Peacock and Tyson quote North Carolina Old Regular Baptist Elder Bradley's assertion "that every time you feel inspired, it didn't necessarily come from the Lord." They comment insightfully: "This habitual suspicion of the human mind is characteristic of Old Baptist psychology, which they exercise as much on themselves as on others. This places the preacher in a position of extreme equivocality. If preaching is the main bridge between the world of scripture and the world of history, spirit, and flesh, then anyone occupying the role of preacher

CHAPTER TWO

both experiences the terror of history and tastes the honey of the Spirit."[26]

They cite another Baptist elder who, attentive to the need for preachers to "prepare the heart" for the homiletical task, began his sermon by saying: "I want to read some scripture that will be found in the second chapter of Ephesians. This scripture seems to linger on my mind. I hope it's of the Lord."[27] Another confessed as he began to preach: "I've carried the weight of a scripture for three months."[28] Again, note the gospel imagery in these descriptions—"prepare the heart," "linger on my mind," "carried the weight of a scripture"—which are the stuff of which sermons are made: oral metaphors that stick in the head, perhaps even the heart, creating what Howard Dorgan calls "mutual response patterns," for preacher and listener alike. Such images shape moments when the audience becomes part of what Dorgan terms "an interactive dynamic process, frequently being moved but also becoming a mover—willingly yielding itself to an organic interplay in which the roles of stimulator and respondent fluctuated between two or more agents." In such cases, Dorgan concludes, "the audience" becomes a "part of an *emotional and spiritual fermentation*, one for which they [are] an essential—and willing—element."[29] With its preacher, the waiting congregation confronts "the terror of history and tastes the honey of the Spirit."[30]

APPALACHIAN PREACHING:
THE GIFTS OF OTHERNESS

Given these dynamics in Appalachian church preaching styles, one might ask: How can this highly regional, almost vanishing tradition, shaped by a specific and perhaps diminishing ecclesiastical context, have meaning not only for urban preaching and preachers, but also in the new Appalachia, filled with Walmarts, megachurches, satellite dishes, and second-home getaways? What's the point of revisiting those "good old-fashioned ways" when they seem to offer at best a limited homiletical praxis for the postmodern church? And on one level those questions are quite valid. The preaching styles, theological systems, and churchly contexts cited here reflect an otherness that today seems quaint, colorful, and distant from our twenty-first-century homiletical circumstances.

Or does it? In his superb, prizewinning volume *Uneven Ground: Appalachia since 1945*, Appalachian scholar Ron Eller comments:

> Appalachia endures as a paradox in American society in part because it plays a critical role in the discourse of national identity but also because the region's struggle with modernity reflects a deeper American failure to define progress in the first place. . . . We *know* that Appalachia exists because we need it to exist in order to define what we are not. The notion of Appalachia as a separate place, a region set off from mainstream culture and history, has allowed us to distance ourselves from the uncomfortable dilemmas that the story of Appalachia raises about our own lives and about the larger society.[31]

Building on this summary of place and margins, let me suggest that Appalachian preaching traditions—eccentricities and all—may be of value because they offer lessons of otherness. Let's be honest: in postmodern America, churches and preachers across the theological spectrum are experiencing serious identity crises (note that I made this plural). Protestant privilege in the culture is dead or dying; church attendance is in serious decline, from the evangelical churches to the mainlines; and in some congregations, the listeners aren't always sure whether the preacher is a real presence or a technology-infused holographic image. Recent polls suggest that "white evangelicals" and non–religiously affiliated persons are neck and neck, at 30 percent of the population each. For many Americans—for example, one in five Millennials, ages eighteen to thirty-five—church in general feels alien and oppressive. So perhaps we have little to lose in listening to the otherness of Appalachian preachers for insights into the gospel we have not considered before. In Appalachian mountain congregations, there are at least four gifts of otherness that might

CHAPTER TWO

aid churches outside the region in rethinking their homiletical and ministerial callings.

First, Appalachian preachers remind us of the otherness of the biblical text, an unpredictability that resists domestication. Again, David Tracy challenges us when he writes: "To encourage interaction between text and interpreter, it is helpful to find examples where the interpreter is forced to recognize otherness by confronting an unexpected claim to truth. So immune can we all become to otherness that we are tempted to reduce all reality to more of the same or to that curious substitute for the same we too often mean when we say similarity."[32] Tracy insists that when considering classic texts such as the Christian Scriptures, the "temptation to domesticate all reality is a temptation that any classic text will resist. The classics resist our ingrained laziness and self-satisfaction. Their claim to attention must be heeded."[33]

Ancient texts resist domestication. Appalachian churches reveal the power of biblical and homiletical oral tradition to nurture religious experience, pass on identity, and, as the hymn says, renew the meaning of the "old, old story of Jesus and his love" in every generation.

Over the years, I've heard Appalachian preachers write themselves and me into the biblical story. Often these preachers had committed to memory large passages of the King James Bible, passed on to them through the oral tradition of other gospel preachers. And the grandeur of their rhetoric drew us in and made us aware of the dangers and demands of the Jesus Story—an undomesticated gospel. Across the years, mountain preachers have made me laugh, cry, and fume, give up unhealthy habits, and take on new ones. Some have quite literally scared the hell out of me with their amazing pulpit prowess while others warmed my heart with the grace of a loving God.

Yet oral tradition is not limited to preaching; it is also integrated into the life and witness of the religious community itself. Deborah McCauley writes insightfully that "this informal—

40

indeed, spontaneous—quality is the creative aspect of traditional religion."[34] Appalachian oral tradition calls us to take seriously the rhetoric of spontaneity and vulnerability, and its capacity to reform the gospel before our very eyes and ears.

Let us ask where we have domesticated the audacious text and in doing so become immune to otherness in the text and in ourselves. When and how does the text compel us to venture into areas of life, thought, and gospel that we have never really considered or where we do not wish to go? Might we, alongside the commentaries, the lectionary blogs, and the preaching workshops, step back and see where the text has taken us, exploring its unexpected earthiness, its assertive women, and its responses to radical justice, compassion, and reconciliation? Appalachian Serpent Handlers taught me this: Sometimes Appalachian preachers (and the rest of us) have been wrong about the text but right about the gospel, and their courage in venturing out on the exegetical ice made me consider the text itself in new ways. John Crowley recounts a conversation with Elder John Harris of the Old Line Suwannee River Association who "said that rather than his taking a text, *the text took him*."[35]

Second, Appalachian preachers reflect the otherness of an enthusiastical faith: a passion for religious experience, what Jonathan Edwards called, "a sense of the heart, of the supreme beauty and sweetness of the holiness or moral perfection of divine things, together with all that discerning knowledge of things of religion that depends upon, and flows from such a sense."[36]

For mountain preachers this "sense of the heart" is anchored in an *experience* of God's grace through faith in Christ, spiritual encounters that must begin in the preacher's own heart. In *Foxfire 7*, Primitive Baptist Howard Parham says of preacher and congregation: "What we do believe in is the preacher getting up there and preaching. But, when he gets to preaching his experiences and my experience, and both of these are alike, then there is where your teaching comes in. He will bring across some points that you haven't thought of. The scripture says, 'teaching and preaching is to stir up your pure mind.' You've already got that pure mind in there; it's just got to be stirred up, and that is one way God has got of doing it.'"[37]

The preacher's task—calling—is to stir up this divine sense of the heart, beginning with his or her own religious experience. Loyal Jones quotes a sermon by Henkle Little, pastor of Calvary Baptist Church, Taylorsville, North Carolina, who says: "It's the most personal thing that's ever happened to me, this thing of salvation. Strange as it may seem to you, I know the salvation of the Lord better than I know my name." Henkle concludes, "I find the people in the Appalachian area, they are people who live closer to the heart of God than most. I can't say what the difference is but they seem to have a more steadfast and surer faith . . . a more burning desire to know the Lord."[38]

Religious experience anchors the preacher, not only in terms of salvation but also in terms of calling. Jones cites Kentucky Primitive Baptist Elder Milford Hall Sr., describing his call to preach. Hall acknowledged that after he was converted, "I was happy again and felt as though I was free forever. . . . But ere long the burden to preach the gospel began to put in its appearance every now and then. This was very obnoxious and terrifying to me. I sought to stifle these thoughts. . . . Finally the 'revelation and appeal' of God was made so plain to me that I was afraid to dilly dally with His grace and put Him off any longer. . . . I could not find a single excuse for any further delay in the matter. It was preach or die."[39]

Even these brief illustrations again reveal what Jonathan Edwards called the "supreme beauty and sweetness of divine things," inherent in a "sense of the heart": "the most personal thing that's ever happened to me"; "this thing of salvation"; "as though I was free forever"; "obnoxious and terrifying"; "afraid to dilly dally" with God's grace; "preach or die." What is it in preaching, any preaching, which helps people feel "free forever?" Whatever our Christian tradition or theology, can we cultivate or deepen an experiential "sense of the heart" that nurtures the spirituality of both transcendence and immanence—the God who is sovereign, "high and lifted up," (Is 6:1) and the God who "became flesh and dwelt among us" (Jn 1:14)? "We need more tenderness now," says Old Regular Baptist Elder Frank Fugate, interviewed in a film made in 1972.[40] We still do.

Third, Appalachian preachers unite sermon and sacrament, the word of God proclaimed and the word of God enacted. They know how to "tangibilify" grace, to use a phrase from Father Divine. Unlike many other evangelical Protestants, they have refused to memorialize the presence of Jesus out of baptism and Holy Communion, and they find Christ's "real presence" in the washing of feet. In religious studies terms, they see preaching as a form of hierophany—the sacred revealed in the ordinary. The "ordinariness of the preacher" who often resists the call like Moses, who claimed he had "uncircumcised lips" (Ex 6:12), and the ordinariness of feet, washed as a sign of love and community (Jn 13:1–5).

In the Appalshop film *In the Good Old Fashioned-Way*, the Old Regular Baptist elder who leads the foot-washing/Communion service does not preach in his own words; instead, he literally chants from the Gospel of John: "And the Lord Jesus, on the night of his arrest, girded himself with a towel and began to wash his disciple's feet." Then he sings the plan of salvation: "By faith we are washed; by faith we are clean." Then the people of God, some of whose hands tremor with age, wash each other's feet. Toward the end of the Communion scene, the preacher sings out triumphantly, "O those feet-washing Baptists, we'll be here till the Lord comes again."[41] Grace tangibilified in bread, wine, and basins of water. As good Calvinists, they know that the spoken word should say what the enacted word means.

The film continues as Old Regular preachers conduct the annual mountainside memorial service, as families gather to clean and leave flowers at the graves of loved ones. The host pastor explains that the tradition dates back to an earlier time when funerals were deferred by mountain families waiting for itinerant preachers to arrive and winter snows to depart. But on that day, what began as a historical tradition becomes a sacramental moment for the little congregation gathered beneath the cemetery arbor. It is an Appalachian hierophany where the sacred appears in the ordinary—for what can be more sacred than a cemetery or more ordinary than death? Hierophany up a hollow.

It is an earthly event—a sermon in the cemetery with temporal, eternal, and eschatological significance. "If," says the preacher, selected to give the sermon by the host pastor only moments before, "If the Lord was to revelate my mind, I might say . . ." Suddenly the Spirit falls, "revelates" his mind, and the sermon begins in a heavenly cadence, a pitch or two higher than his "earthly" voice.

With cremation increasingly normative, what new hierophantic vision does twenty-first-century preaching need to pursue? How can gospel spirituality be tangibilified in a culture where fewer and fewer people know why Christians find outward and visible signs of inward and spiritual grace in water, bread, wine, oil, and damp towels?

The Appalachian mountain churches remind us of the historic and immediate links between sacrament, life, and death. In the baptismal immersion they practice, usually in flowing creeks and rivers, the baptismal formula includes phrases such as "buried with Christ in baptism, raised to walk in newness of life." River baptism itself is a reminder that if the preacher holds the new convert a little too long under the water or if the currents are too strong, eternity might come quicker than anticipated. Likewise, at Holy Communion the congregation recalls Jesus's words at the table: "This is my body, which is given for you" (Lk 22:19)—words of life and death, body and blood. On that same first-century night, Jesus tells his disciples, "If I then, your Lord and Teacher, have washed your feet, you also ought to wash one another's feet" (Jn 13:14). Even if those words are not taken literally, they are surely a call to compassionate action by those who claim the Jesus Story. Appalachian mountain churches are, in their words, a witness to the truth of these life and death issues and actions.

Finally, Appalachian preachers pass along the gift of audacious rhetoric, intent on awakening the church and the churchly from indifference, insensitivity, and spiritual callousness. John Crowley notes that in 1833, the Ochlocknee Association of Georgia Primitive Baptists encouraged its ministers to preach "to the consolation of mourners, the establishment of saints, and the alarming of sinners."[42] This approach was proclamation directed to pastoral care, Christian maturity, and the awakening of sinners to the dangers of hell and the benefits of salvation. Crowley cites two twentieth-century Primitive Baptist preachers, Elders Marcus Peavy and Fred Bethea, who testified to having undergone "something similar to a visionary experience while preaching, as though they saw their subject unrolling before their eyes." Crowley recounts another Primitive Baptist elder who told of hearing a "more polished" mountain homiletician offer a sermon in which he "deliberately broke himself of chanting in the pulpit," to which an old-time Baptist elder responded: "And he broke himself of preaching, too."[43]

In Appalachia, all sorts of preachers get called to awaken the church. In 1988 some students who were studying with us in the Appalachian Ministries Educational Resource Center summer program based in Berea, Kentucky, interviewed Sister Lydia Surgener, a Holiness preacher who ran a used clothing store in Pennington Gap, Virginia. Sister Lydia found her own sacred space, a deserted Pentecostal church building near Cranks Creek, Kentucky, and decided to resurrect it. That church wasn't dead, Sister Lydia said; it was just asleep! God told her to wake it up, so she went there on Sundays and started preaching, with only her nephew, Junior, as the congregation. Gradually other people joined them, and the church woke up.

When I gave the fall Christianity Lectures at Berea College in 2010, I mentioned Sister Lydia's efforts. After I returned home, the Berea campus chaplain, Jeff Pool, received a visit from a stu-

CHAPTER TWO

dent who identified himself as Sister Lydia's great nephew. He was present at the lecture and told Dr. Pool to let me know that his "auntie" had passed away but that her church was still "awake."

Appalachian preachers would be the first to admit that the "foolishness of the preaching of the cross" (cf. 1 Cor 1:18, KJV) haunts them. But sometimes they venture out on the homiletical ice to see where the text will take them, empowered by the audacious and terrifying possibility that preachers really might say something that carries preacher and listener toward a "sense of the heart" beyond their wildest gospel imaginations. If the nineteenth-century preachers were correct, then sometimes it is not that we take the text but that the text takes us. Sometimes the text really does overtake us, sending our most treasured doctrines and traditions into a tailspin. Sister Lydia Surgener started preaching to an audience of one, waiting on the Spirit to awaken some sacred space long fallen into silence. Surely there can be no more heart-cheering, affecting, and transforming sermon than that, inside or outside the hills and hollows of Appalachia.

CHAPTER 3

Revisiting the "Woman's Sphere"

Implicit and Explicit Feminism
in Appalachian Churches

In 1988, I began teaching in the summer program of the Appalachian Ministries Educational Resource Center (AMERC), a consortium of seminaries and divinity schools founded by Helen Lewis and Mary Lee Daugherty to provide "experiential learning" in the Appalachian region. The program brought theology students from diverse Catholic and Protestant institutions to Berea, Kentucky, for several weeks of study and travel, credited by their respective institutions. Student housing and classes took place on the campus of Berea College, but on weekends, they were assigned to churches, community agencies, and farm families for "immersion experiences" in neighboring counties.

Mary Lee Daugherty, who first envisioned the Appalachian ministry program, sought to introduce ministerial students to the history, sociology, theology, and praxis of Christian communions in Appalachia. Daugherty died in 2005, but AMERC continues by funding courses in Appalachian religion for member schools.[1]

Helen Lewis, called by many "the mother of Appalachian Studies," was an insightful analyst of Appalachian life and culture with an amazing network of scholars and community activists with whom she partnered in empowering grassroots individuals and agencies while also addressing, often confronting, the power brokers in academia, corporations, and city halls. Helen died in 2022, but her work and her witness for justice in Appalachia endures.[2]

47

CHAPTER THREE

SISTER LYDIA SURGENER: PERSONIFYING THE WOMAN'S SPHERE IN APPALACHIA

During my first summer in the AMERC program, a group of students did their experiential learning in Pennington Gap, Virginia, visiting churches and community programs. While there, they interviewed Sister Lydia Surgener—referenced in the previous chapter—a Pentecostal preacher and proprietor of a used clothing store in Pennington Gap. References to her and her work appear throughout this book. The interview was conducted on a hot summer's day in the un-air-conditioned clothing store, and amid the heat, the students noted, "Sister Lydia didn't sweat," a phenomenon they attributed to her complete immersion in the Holy Ghost!

Sister Lydia was an evangelist, an office which Holiness-Pentecostal churches have long opened to women. Her life and ideas are documented in Deborah McCauley's *Appalachian Mountain Religion*. McCauley writes: "For independent Holiness churches, the path made up of personal qualities, the apprenticeship of experience, and communal recognition is usually understood to be all that is necessary for the 'ordination' of Holiness preachers such as Sister Lydia, whose religious authority and communal standing no one disputes. Upon occasion, preachers may gather, formally or informally, to lay hands on a brother or sister in recognition of their ministry, although this step is in no way a requirement."[3]

Sister Lydia, now deceased, illustrates something of the paradox of women's "place" or "sphere" in Appalachian independent Pentecostal churches. Her gifts were readily recognized as those that were "poured out on all flesh" when the Holy Spirit fell at Pentecost. Her "religious authority and communal standing" were indisputable. Yet although she functioned as an evangelist, freely preaching the gospel, she was not allowed to serve as pastor, since that would challenge the literalistic interpretations of certain New Testament passages.

McCauley comments:

> Mountain women would always have a prominent place in their religious culture, although limitations would vary from one mountain church tradition to another. Their "liberties" ranged from freedom to voice their own spontaneous, ecstatic expressions; to praying aloud and testifying; to preaching in many independent Holiness churches (as well as in the rural mountain churches of the Church of God [Cleveland, Tennessee], or on the local radio or at revivals. Women also serve as caretakers of church houses or may be the prime movers in starting up a church; finally a woman may achieve the nearly unchallengeable authority of a church "matriarch" (a term not used by mountain people)—a position associated with age, wisdom, and outstanding spiritual maturity.[4]

THE "WOMAN'S SPHERE" IN APPALACHIAN CHURCHES

Appalachian Holiness and Baptist congregations perpetuate the concept of what is sometimes known as the "woman's sphere," a willingness to assign women various roles in the church and the home while setting boundaries that limit their leadership and calling to wider participation in church offices and ordained ministries. Inside the woman's sphere Appalachian females have developed significant leadership and power in specific congregations—teaching children and other women, funding programs, engaging in various missionary and benevolent activities and often in serving as the largest segment of the Sunday and weekday life of the church. If they step out of those boundaries, however, women may experience sanctions or even expulsion from the congregation that rejects their public leadership.

University of North Carolina historian Donald Mathews notes that, especially in the South, the woman's sphere was "a model of behavior and ideals which was peculiarly the possession of women and was based on their unique contribution to the ideal community."[5] Women were thus assigned or encouraged to exercise their spiritual gifts in ways that did not challenge the literal interpretation of certain New Testament texts. They were the models of virtue, nurture, and a special spirituality not given to males. Mathews observes: "It was almost as if men willingly conceded the moral superiority of women in order to prevent active female participation in worldly [and churchly] affairs."[6] As new generations of women moved toward ordination and the ministry, they challenged this reading of Scripture and its accompanying "sphere" in ways that often brought them into conflict with those who continued to insist that the Bible prohibits women from pastoral office and function.

In a sense, the evolution of women to the ordained ministry came as they moved beyond a limited "sphere" to a broader understanding of God's call upon all human beings. It began earlier in colonial American history, with women like Margaret Meuse Clay, charged with "unlicensed preaching" in Virginia in 1770.[7] Participation in the nineteenth-century frontier revivals led many other women to exercise gifts of proclamation and religious fervor.

Christine Leigh Heyrman writes that early in the awakenings many Baptist and Methodist preachers supported the idea "that women of all ages and races might exercise their gifts by speaking before public, sexually mixed, religious gatherings. Thereby the clergy endorsed the view that acceptable forms of female spiritual expression went beyond fulfilling their private roles as dutiful wives, mothers, and sisters."[8] They went beyond the woman's sphere. However, Heyrman's research led her to conclude that many ministers came to reject this larger role for females in Protestant churches, fearing that the churches would become the near exclusive domain of women, and men would turn away in droves.[9]

The tradition of women participating in public discourse, even preaching, is not new in Appalachia. Elder John Sparks documents the controversy that arose from time to time among eighteenth-century Separate Baptists in North Carolina and Kentucky regarding the practice of women "testifying" in public worship services. One particular culprit was Martha Stearns Marshall, sister of Shubal Stearns and wife of Daniel Marshall, two preachers who, in 1755, founded the Sandy Creek Church, the first Baptist church in the North Carolina backcountry. Sparks writes that "after 1747 [their wedding date] Marshall and his young wife began a phenomenally active *joint ministry* [italics mine] that would endure through nearly forty years of labor together, the births of several children, and countless ups and downs." Her preaching to both men and women apparently caused grave concern among some Baptist brethren.[10]

MOUNTAIN CHURCHES
AND WOMEN'S ORDINATION

The Holiness-Pentecostals

The Church of God, Cleveland, Tennessee, founded in in 1886 in Monroe County, has long had female evangelists, even pastors. Cheryl Bridges Johns, professor of discipleship and Christian formation at Pentecostal Theological Seminary, the denomination's flagship school for ministers, notes, "The holiness churches were the first to see that the issue of slavery and that of women were to be read with the same scriptural hermeneutic, namely that in Christ there was established the seed bed for restoration of a new order of humanity in which slaves were liberated and women set free. For that reason, the churches out of the holiness revival have always given women full liberty as administrators, pastors, teachers."

Johns was particularly concerned when, in 2010, representatives at the church's seventy-third annual conference ruled by a fifty-eight-vote majority that women, although ordained to pastoral ministry, would not be permitted to be ordained as bishops or serve on governing councils.[11]

The International Pentecostal Holiness Church (IPHC), founded in North Carolina in 1911, grew out of the Holiness and Pentecostal revivals of the late nineteenth and early twentieth centuries. Women have served as preachers and evangelists in the Appalachian Conference of the IPHC from the beginning. In 2019, the General Superintendent's Report of the Appalachian Conference observed: "The Appalachian Conference is leading the way in recognizing women who are called to ministry. In its early years, the conference welcomed and supported female missionaries like Fannie Lowe, the IPHC's first medical missionary to Hong Kong, and multiple women evangelists. Today, the conference has a record 106 credentialed women—nearly 25% of their total ministers—including 22 women serving as senior pastors, co-pastors, or full-time staff at larger churches."[12]

Mountain Baptists and Women's Ordination

And then there are the Baptists. Few, if any, traditional Baptist subdenominations—Primitive, Old Regular, Regular, United, or Southern Baptist—permit the ordination of females, let alone allow them to preach or pastor. Churches in the Southern Baptist Convention (SBC), the largest Protestant denomination in both the United States and Appalachia, are quite specific about the ecclesiastical parameters for women as based in their biblical interpretations. The denominational confession of faith, known as the Baptist Faith and Message, first approved in 1925, revised in 1963 and 2000, contains a statement that, while recognizing the significant role that women play in all SBC churches, repudiates the ordination of women for the pastoral office. As revised in 2000, the confession states: "While both men and women are gifted for service in the church, the office of pastor is limited to men as qualified by Scripture."[13]

For the SBC, inside and outside Appalachia, what was once a local church decision has become a denominational article of faith. Before this tightening of theological and congregational restrictions, numerous Southern Baptist churches ordained women, the first such event occurring in 1964 when Addie Davis was ordained by Watts Street Baptist Church in Durham, North Carolina. Twenty-first-century SBC-affiliated churches that conduct such ordinations are now subject to expulsion by the denomination.

In February 2023, the SBC excluded Saddleback Valley Church, the second-largest SBC congregation, from the denomination because it ordained several women and called a female co-pastor.[14]

Independent Baptists are even more specific. The Articles of Faith of the Baptist Bible Fellowship International, an organization of Independent Baptist churches, summarize the twofold approach of many Baptist groups inside and outside Appalachia regarding the role of women in the church. It states: "We believe that men and women are spiritually equal in position before God but that God has ordained distinct and separate spiritual functions of men and women in the home and in the church. The husband is to be the leader of the home and men are to hold the leadership positions (pastors and deacons) in the church. Accordingly, only men are eligible of licensure and ordination for pastor by the church."[15] While claiming a spiritual equality of both men and women "before God," these Baptists close the door to any consideration of females as pastors or deacons.

Commenting on the practices of the Appalachian-based Fellowship Independent Baptist Church, ethnomusicologist Jeff Todd Titon writes:

> For example, it seemed to me that some of the women chafed under the church's patriarchal rules. The deacons and minister must be male; the songleader was male; prayers always were led by males; outside of participation in Sunday school and in testimony before singing a special or after the sermon, a woman could not speak to the congregation during the worship service. . . . At the same time, it was clear that some of the women in the congregation had considerable verbal gifts and, when impressed to do so by the Spirit, did not hesitate to use them.[16]

In his studies of the mountain Baptist "sub-denominations," Howard Dorgan notes that the early tradition in many Primitive and Old Regular Baptist churches placed emphasis on the strict separation of the sexes in worship. Women were not allowed to preach or in many cases even speak in public worship (unless shouting in the power of the Spirit). Some Old Regular congre-

CHAPTER THREE

gations forbid women to wear slacks, have "bobbed hair" or "officiate in any official capacity of the church."[17] Certain churches separate men and women on opposite sides of the church and some even maintained separate entrances for men and women into the building.[18]

"I SUFFER NOT A WOMAN": THE BIBLE AND THE "WOMAN'S SPHERE"

Dorgan illustrates the way in which this indirect influence takes shape in Old Regular Baptist life. He cites Elder Atlas Hall, who observed:

> Among those churches which permit female members to be a clerk or treasurer, and even in the Mountain Association which permits female delegates, the sisters still refrain from taking part in the actual discussion or debate of items of business. The sisters will reserve their comments or opinions for discussion after the council meeting. At that time, they will often give their opinions or views, and if they can convince (and generally they can), the males will ratify an action at a future church council which the females are not in agreement with, thus being assured that their participation is acceptable and appreciated.

Elder Hall cites numerous biblical texts he believes dictate women's silence in the church.[19]

Such a position is echoed, formally or informally, by many Appalachian denominations and churches. Indeed, even those groups that accept or encourage the ordination of women and their presence on ministerial staffs often remain hesitant to call women as senior pastors.

While women have always played vital roles in Appalachian churches and continue to represent the largest constituency in Appalachian faith, many mountain congregations, both Protestant and Catholic, maintain specific hermeneutical and cultural methods for defining the role of women in the church, the family, and the larger society, as we will see in the sections that follow.

REVISITING THE "WOMAN'S SPHERE"

The Doctrine of Complementarity

A literalist hermeneutic led most Appalachian men (and many women) to believe that females were excluded from ordained ministry, "subject" to the authority of their husbands (or fathers) in matters spiritual and familial, and in many cases forbidden to teach males beyond the age of twelve. Today, this interpretation is known as the doctrine of complementarity, in which men and women are considered spiritually equal by their redemption in Christ but are assigned specific roles on the basis of God's created order.

Biblical texts are cited as mandating women's exclusion from ordained ministry and defining their roles in family and church, including:

> Let the woman learn in silence with all subjection. But I suffer not a woman to teach, nor to usurp authority over the man, but to be in silence. For Adam was first formed, then Eve. And Adam was not deceived, but the woman being deceived was in the transgression." (1 Tim 2:11–14, KJV)

> Wives, submit yourselves unto your own husbands, as unto the Lord. For the husband is the head of the wife, even as Christ is head of the church: and he is the saviour of the body. Therefore as the church is subject unto Christ, so let the wives be to their own husbands in everything." (Eph 5:22–24, KJV)

Twentieth-century Tennessee Independent Baptist leader John R. Rice was among the most literal of the biblical literalists in asserting the essential maleness of the Divine and the church. In a sermon addressed "to men only," Rice declared that "God is a masculine God. A man, then, is nearer like God than a woman, and in a sense, man is in the image of God. . . . The Bible plainly says that Eve was deceived but that Adam was not deceived. He knew better. He knew it would not make him wise. God never intended women to lead men around by their noses. . . . Men are to lead out in music, in Bible teaching in the church, in personal soul winning in the church. . . . God has reserved the main place in the church

CHAPTER THREE

for men."[20] These words, though extreme, characterize the way in which many traditional Appalachian churches continue to understand the role of women in home and congregation.

Toward a Theology of Women in Ministry

Mainline ecumenical denominations (generally) offer more progressive interpretations. These Appalachian Christian communities affirm that the New Testament describes multiple possibilities for considering women as full participants in the ordained leadership of churches. Unlike John R. Rice, they note that Adam was the one with the weak spiritual DNA, agreeing with the last person or serpent he talked to, even blaming God for his own wrong decision in the garden. Caught in sin, Adam blamed both God and Eve: "And the man said, 'The woman whom thou gavest to be with me, she gave me of the tree, and I did eat'" (Gen 3:12, KJV).

Progressive Appalachian churches challenge those views by citing texts such as Romans 8:1–3, applied to all persons who are "in Christ": "There is therefore now no condemnation to them which are in Christ Jesus. . . . For the law of the Spirit of life in Christ Jesus hath made me free from the law of sin and of death" (KJV). Likewise, at Pentecost the Holy Spirit is poured out upon "all flesh," thereby enabling men and women to "prophesy" and declare the good news (Acts 2:17). Paul concludes, "For as many of you as have been baptized into Christ have put on Christ. There is neither Jew nor Greek, there is neither bond nor free, there is neither male nor female: for ye are all one in Christ Jesus" (Gal 3:27–28, KJV). On this issue, like others, Appalachian Protestants continue to debate the way they read and use biblical texts.

CATHOLIC WOMEN IN APPALACHIA: THE FOCIS COMMUNITY

The woman's sphere among Catholics in Appalachia is poignantly evident in the actions of the Glenmary Sisters in Big Stone Gap,

Virginia, in 1967. Their pilgrimage is documented in the book *Mountain Sisters*, written by Helen Lewis and Monica Appleby and incorporating essays and interviews with numerous women involved in the order.

The missionary order of the Glenmary Sisters was founded in 1941 by Father William Howard Bishop and given Rome's canonical approval in 1952, primarily to serve in rural areas in the United States. The first sisters came to Appalachia in 1947, charged with missionizing in the region. Father Bishop advised them accordingly:

> You must acquire Christian-like love for the poor and a great desire to minister to them. You must win them by your kindness in relieving their suffering. You must be careful that you never make them feel inferior by flaunting your superiority or by unkindness in any way. They must see your love for Christ and your sincerity in trying to help them. You will see suffering of every kind among these people and your hearts will go out to them. You will minister to their bodily needs and win their confidence. Then you can speak to them about Jesus, Mary, and Joseph, the ideal family who were poor and who suffered.[21]

Father Bishop set the boundaries of their mission—to collaborate with the Appalachian people to "win their confidence" and then deliver the story of Jesus to them. But something happened in the hills and hollows of Appalachia. As Rosemary Radford Reuther writes: "Instead of converting the mountain people to Catholicism, the Sisters were evangelized by the mountain families. The Sisters had carried out a 'religious survey' asking questions of mountain men and women about their beliefs and their faith. They were reeducated by mountain theologians and were 'baptized' in the mountains, 'converted' by Appalachia."[22]

Suffice it to say that the Sisters sought to "align" a "ministry to the Appalachian people" that, in their words, was "intended to cut across existing lines and divisions—religious, class, racial, educational, cultural, political, etc.—to bring about an experience of social integration or community."[23] This inevitably brought them into

CHAPTER THREE

conflict with the Church hierarchy who saw their actions as outside the proper "sphere" for Catholic sisters. As Lenore Mullarney, a Glenmary sister, wrote:

> Here we were, about a hundred of us, young people, eager to go and do. The archbishop once thought we were great because we were alive and open to suggestion. We were really kind of the darlings for awhile. But deciding the internal rules by which everyone will be governed, now that's the society's prerogative. When someone else comes in and starts telling you when to go to bed, that's too much. When you enter a society, that's the understanding that the Sisters control the living situation. You wouldn't do anything public contrary to the church. We finally felt we had done what we could.[24]

Mountain Sisters documents the 1967 departure of some of the women from the order and their creation of the Federation of Communities in Service (FOCIS), an organization for continued vocation in the mountains but outside the Catholic Church. Their story is something of a "Catholic take" on the conflicts that can develop when women step outside the specified sphere for ministry, vocation, and identity.

CIRCLE OF MERCY CONGREGATION:
EXPANDING THE WOMAN'S SPHERE

Transitions in the Appalachian woman's sphere were evident to faculty and students working in the AMERC multicultural immersion experience in Madison County, North Carolina, in January 2007. During that winter course students met a variety of women doing ministry in traditional and nontraditional roles. Several students shadowed a local Episcopal woman who was pastor of a rural church in the county. The entire group attended the Circle of Mercy congregation in Asheville, a Baptist-oriented congregation served by male/female co-pastors. They also met with a panel of women that included a member of the FOCIS community, which came out of the Glenmary Sisters in the 1960s. An ordained minister, she had recently been released from six weeks of incarcera-

58

tion that resulted from her participation in peace actions against the war in Iraq. Another woman on the panel described her work as a hospice chaplain in Madison County. A recent seminary graduate, the middle-aged woman acknowledged that while she might have sought ordination, she chose not to do so since her mountain Baptist church was very traditional and "not ready for ordained women" as yet.

Two Methodist women on the panel, both sisters, confessed that they were "mountain women" serving in various lay capacities in their church, a rural congregation dealing with transitions related to changing population patterns, the building of innumerable condominiums all around them, and the growth of the "second home" phenomenon in the region. Their church was not adapting to those realities well, they reported, but women were working in lay ministries nonetheless.

APPALACHIAN WOMEN IN MINISTRY: FACING THE FUTURE

What does the future hold for Appalachian women in ministry? The possibilities might include the following.

First, Appalachian denominations and congregations remain divided over the very nature of ordination and pastoral ministry for women. For many churches, acceptance of women as ordained pastors would require a change in biblical interpretation that they are unwilling or unable to make, fostering a reevaluation of their entire biblical hermeneutic, with implications for other doctrines and practices. For these groups, the woman's sphere is grounded in the divine order of creation in the church and the world.

Second, some Appalachian churches and denominations continue to place the issue of women in ministry within the context of the woman's sphere in subjection to God and to males, especially fathers, husbands, and pastors. From their perspective women's leadership roles in church and family are clearly proscribed in

Scripture. Feminism, women's work outside the home, ordination of women, and other efforts to step outside the sphere are seen as evidence of the "last days," a prelude to the return of Jesus Christ. One Appalachian Independent Baptist church affirms this doctrinal statement: "It is exceedingly dangerous for a woman to get out of her orbit. God never created woman to rule man. His whole Word is against it. Because of this broken law the curse of God is on the home, church, society, and nation."[25]

Many Appalachian Christians, men and women alike, feel strongly that the mandated role of each of the sexes must not be violated. They believe that women's attempts to usurp the power of men in home or pulpit represent a direct challenge to the divinely ordained authority and order of the church.

Third, certain denominationally based churches in the region—Presbyterians, Episcopalians, Lutherans, and United Methodists, and progressive Baptists—have ordained women and placed them in churches throughout Appalachia. While most of these pastors are in towns or urban areas, there are also some rural congregations that have received women as pastors or staff members—not without controversy. Yet if recent surveys and studies are any indication, the road to a senior pastorate remains extremely difficult for ordained women in Appalachia. While there are signs that a growing number of churches are revisiting the issue through their pastoral search committees, the willingness of churches even to consider female candidates for a pastorate often remains the exception, not the norm.

Finally, Appalachian church leaders would do well to acknowledge that the movement of women toward pastoral ministry or at least to functions outside the traditional woman's sphere is in large part due to the spirituality and piety of their respective faith communities. Young women grow up under the "nurture and admonition" of the church, often being told to do whatever God tells them to do, to follow the Holy Spirit wherever it may take them. But when they take their elders at their word and do just that, moving toward responses to Christian calling and vocation, some of their leaders warn that they are going too far. Piety broke the barriers of the woman's sphere long before feminism even appeared on the horizon.

WHEN GOSPEL OTHERNESS PREVAILS: A CASE STUDY

There are times, however, when the spirituality of otherness and Christian nurture forces even the preachers to live out their own rhetoric. The Reverend Harold McKinnish, who died in 2014, was the personification of a mountain preacher, serving Baptist churches in places like Bat Cave and Tuxedo, North Carolina, for six decades. He married and buried thousands of people across sixty years of Appalachian ministry. When he died, several thousand people attended what became a five-hour wake the night before his funeral.

Years before, when Rev. McKinnish's twelve-year-old daughter Linda blurted out: "Daddy, why can't women preach?" He responded: "Because God didn't ordain it." Yet when he kept preaching, "Do whatever God calls you to do," Linda finally took him at his word. She went to the Southern Baptist Theological Seminary, Louisville, Kentucky, receiving the Master of Divinity, and then, with her husband, Tilden Bridges, became a Baptist missionary to Taiwan, later returning to the seminary for a PhD in New Testament.

When Linda McKinnish Bridges got ordained to the gospel ministry, the Reverend Harold decided she was "God-called" and celebrated her call to preach. At her PhD graduation he wept uncontrollably.

Invited to teach Greek at the seminary amid the infamous SBC controversy between "Conservatives" and "Moderates," McKinnish Bridges was eventually told that her contract would not be renewed due to conservative opposition to an ordained woman teaching the Bible to men.

When her final semester ended, Brother Harold drove his truck from North Carolina to Louisville to help her empty her seminary office, but before he would let them leave the campus, he compelled her to kneel with him in front of the school's administration building, take off their shoes, and shake the dust of the place off their feet. The Reverend Dr. McKinnish Bridges calls their action a "sacrament of failure," which took her beyond anger and bitterness.

Thus the woman's sphere was transformed because a father's enthusiastical mountain rhetoric "tangibilified" grace in ways that transformed father and daughter alike. His biblicism set her free when her alma mater stopped being *mater*, but her call to preach freed him, too—a long way from that Sunday when she was twelve. Father proclaimed an audacious mountain gospel, and taking him at his word, daughter made that gospel more audacious than he ever imagined. Ultimately, the Holy Spirit and the spirituality of otherness overwhelmed them both.

It can happen like that, in the Appalachian Mountains, by grace.

CHAPTER 4

Otherness on the Margins

Pentecostal Serpent Handlers
and "No Heller" Primitive Baptists

AT A SERPENT HANDLING

I attended my first serpent handling in June 1990. It was a celebrative affair—a kind of family reunion, dinner on the ground, revival meeting, and serpent handling all rolled into one. It occurred on a sultry Sunday morning up a hollow, not far from Kentucky's Berea College. The service was outdoors, the best place for a first encounter. It began with a communal prayer with everybody kneeling on the hard ground, many praying aloud simultaneously. Then came the singing, accompanied by guitars and tambourines.

Then the sermons. First up was a young man preaching his heart out but struggling to get his gospel point across. His listeners encouraged him mightily, calling out Bible texts and amens, urging him on. He gave it all he had but was going nowhere, and everybody knew it. Finally, in desperation, a woman in the crowd called out: "Hep him Jesus, hep him." Well, even Jesus couldn't "hep him" that day, so some of the women picked up guitars and started singing, and the young man knew his time was up, deferring to a more seasoned preacher. I learned later that the women were "singing him down," a firm but caring way a congregation reminded a struggling preacher it was time to sit down.[1]

Georgia preacher Brother Byron took it from there, denouncing sin and offering the promise of deliverance, taking no theolog-

CHAPTER FOUR

ical prisoners. Suddenly he walked over to a wooden box, flipped open the lid, and lifted up the biggest timber rattlesnake I had ever seen. There he stood, preaching the gospel, and wrestling a serpent right before our very eyes. It was amazing, overpowering, and terrifying. "I don't fear this serpent more than I would a little bitty baby," Brother Byron said.

Astounded by the experience, I recounted the event in my fall church history class at the Baptist seminary in Louisville where I was then teaching. Several weeks later we were discussing the theology of Saint Thomas Aquinas, whose ontological argument for God's existence gave the class particular difficulty. I struggled to get the point across, and in desperation, a student shouted from the back of the room: "Well, hep him, Jesus, hep him." Class dismissed. Such assistance is no less necessary in attempting to describe the Appalachian Serpent Handlers and Primitive Baptist Universalists.

HERMENEUTICS ON THE MARGINS

In this chapter, we confront the spirituality of otherness in two small but fascinating Appalachian religious groups, the Serpent-Handling Pentecostals and the Primitive Baptist Universalists (so-called "No Hellers"), who reside at either end of the Appalachian theological spectrum. Unique to Appalachia, both carry their interpretations of Christian Scriptures to their logical—some critics would say, illogical—conclusions. While the theology and practice in each group is important for itself, the ways in which both communions came to those beliefs could have significant implications for the Christian community at large. Both the Serpent Handlers and the Baptist Universalists came out of denominations with distinctive Protestant orthodoxies. They simply expanded those beliefs with their own distinctive biblical and theological analyses.

Their biblical interpretations (hermeneutics is the technical term) reflect their unique use of the biblical text. Both groups illus-

64

trate University of Chicago theologian David Tracy's assertion that ancient texts resist "domestication." As noted in an earlier chapter, Tracy writes that our "temptation to domesticate all reality is a temptation that any classic text will resist. The classics resist our ingrained laziness and self-satisfaction. Their claim to attention must be heeded."[2]

The beliefs of Appalachian Serpent Handlers and the Baptist Universalists offer insights into biblical interpretations that may inform the nature of faith and spirituality in the larger Christian community. Tracy suggests that "anyone can also learn interpretation theories (or hermeneutics). Then we may use these theories as they should be used: as further practical skills for the central task of becoming human."[3] Serpent Handlers resist textual "domestication" by their very literal reading of Mark 16:17–19 ("They shall take up serpents," Jesus says) in ways that move beyond the accepted Holiness-Pentecostal approaches to those verses. Primitive Baptist Universalists challenge, or reinterpret, John Calvin's classic biblical interpretations of election, predestination, limited atonement, total depravity, and eternal damnation by insisting that the love of God and the sacrifice of Jesus Christ are so spiritually redemptive that no one gets left behind.

APPALACHIAN DISSENTERS

In both of these Christian traditions, Serpent-Handling and Primitive Baptist Universalism, their conflicting biblical interpretations constitute a form of dissent in response to traditional Baptist and Pentecostal orthodoxy. According to the American Dictionary, dissent means "a strong difference of opinion on a particular subject, especially about an official suggestion."[4]

In *Dissent in American Religion*, historian Edwin Scott Gaustad lays out an imperative of dissent in the cause of justice, writing, "Should a society [whether church or state] actually succeed . . . in suffocating all contrary opinion, then its own vital juices no longer flow and the shadow of death begins to fall across it. No society—ecclesiastical or political, military or literary—can afford to be snared by its own slogans."[5]

Dissenters compound faith's eccentricities and call attention to the ways in which governments and religious communities may cut deals with their consciences for the sake of order and control. Gaustad notes: "This reform of religion in the name of religion, this growing edge, this refusal to let well enough alone, is the role of dissent." Such gospel edginess, he says, "may also be a manifestation of the unfettered human spirit."[6]

Gaustad insists, "The dissenter is a powerful if unpredictable engine in the service of a cause."[7] Dissent is most often a minority response to the dominant political, religious, and cultural majority. Dissenters provide a witness to alternative visions that challenge the "normative" order of things.

The "otherness" evident in Serpent-Handling Pentecostals and in Primitive Baptist Universalists reflects two unique forms of dissent within Appalachian Christian traditions. In a sense, the spirituality of otherness each group cultivates is also a reflection of their dissent against the biblical and doctrinal orthodoxy of the Appalachian Christian traditions from which they come.

APPALACHIAN SERPENT HANDLERS: ULTIMATE BIBLICAL INERRANTISTS?

Serpent-Handling churches are unique to Appalachia. They grew out of the Holiness-Pentecostal movement that took formal shape around 1906 and today is one of the most popular forms of Christianity worldwide. Like all Protestant evangelicals, Serpent Handlers are conversionists, who insist that all persons who claim membership in Christ's church must experience a work of grace in their hearts through faith in Christ. Yet for Pentecostals, the "full gospel" also requires the baptism of the Holy Spirit, a sanctifying experience evidenced by glossolalia, speaking in tongues.

Interpreting Mark 16

Serpent Handlers part company with evangelicals and Pentecostals in their reading of Mark 16:17–19, which is a central focus of their doctrine and religious experience. The text itself is problematic in that it is sometimes referred to as the "false ending" or "long ending" of Mark's Gospel, a segment not found in some of the earliest New Testament manuscripts and thought to have been added in the second century.[8] Serpent Handlers, however, assert that if God had not wanted it in the biblical text, it would not have appeared there.

The King James Version translates the Markan passage: "And these signs shall follow them that believe; in my name shall they cast out devils; they shall speak with new tongues; they shall take up serpents; and if they drink any deadly thing, it shall not hurt them; they shall lay hands on the sick, and they shall recover. So then after the Lord had spoken unto them, he was received up into heaven, and sat on the right hand of God. And they went forth, and preached everywhere, the Lord working with them, and confirming the word with signs following." Most Pentecostals practice three of the five gifts of the Spirit found in those verses—casting out demons, speaking with "new tongues," and laying hands on the sick for healing. Yet Serpent Handlers alone "take up" the dreaded reptiles and, on occasion, drink poison (a "deadly thing"), when, the believers contend, the "anointing" of the Spirit seizes them.

Serpent handling often seems the ultimate biblical literalism, a practice born around 1909 within the early Pentecostal Church of God tradition when Holiness preacher George Hensley first took up serpents in east Tennessee churches.

Their serpent handling is inseparable from their belief, shared with evangelicals and Pentecostals, that the Bible is inerrant, totally trustworthy in every topic it covers. By "confirming the word" through serpent handling, these believers insist they are validating Scripture for the rest of the church. By taking up ser-

CHAPTER FOUR

pents, they authenticate the gospel of Jesus Christ as set forth in an unerring Bible. "Gaining victory over the serpent" verifies the power of God by faith.

When participants are bitten, as many are, or die, then the fault is not with God but with the believer whose faith was not strong enough or who did not receive the anointing of the Spirit. When all else fails, they say the bite of the serpent was simply "the will of God." Few seek medical attention when bitten, trusting God's will to see them through or send them to eternity.[9]

Elzie Preast, a West Virginia Serpent Handler, explained: "But it does say, 'They shall take up serpents.' And Jesus is the one's doing the talking. Said, 'They shall take them up.' Well, I've got to do it, or somebody's got to do it, or else it makes Jesus out a liar, because if I tell you shall go out that door, it means that you've got to go out there, one way or the other. . . . If we don't do it, Jesus can raise up a people that will do it."[10]

Assessing Serpent Handlers' Biblicism

Numerous scholars provide varying analyses of the serpent-handling phenomenon, investigating its spirituality, its geographic and sociological context, and its particular biblical interpretations.

In a 1998 article in the *International Journal for the Psychology of Religion*, Ralph W. Hood, psychology professor at University of Tennessee, Chattanooga, wrote: "They are a deviant [dissenting] religious sect with importance both for the scientific study of religion and for the theological implications of their beliefs and practices."[11] In *Serpent-Handling Believers*, Tom Burton, professor of Appalachian studies at East Tennessee State University, suggests: "They may be said to be achieving an epiphany, that is, an intuitive grasp of reality, a perception of the essential nature or the meaning of themselves, religion, and God. They go to the serpent box for truth; and they believe that, not to be harmed, they have to be filled with the power of God, inspired, fully anointed with divinity."[12]

Mary Lee Daugherty, founder of the Appalachian Ministries

OTHERNESS ON THE MARGINS

Educational Resource Center, concluded that serpent handling had salvific implications for participants, a "sacrament" that is alive and can kill you, as Christian worship becomes a literal matter of life and death.[13] Serpent Handlers understand this reality, recognizing that some practitioners have been or will be "serpent-bitten" in the act of worship. Although an actual number is difficult to secure, in 2014, Paul Williamson, professor of psychology at Henderson State University, reported having documented some ninety-one deaths that had occurred since the movement's origins in 1909.[14]

In *Taking Up Serpents: Snake Handlers of Eastern Kentucky*, David Kimbrough describes a serpent-handling service as he experienced it. The service began with singing, accompanied by cymbals, tambourines, guitars, and other musical instruments. Then, Kimbrough writes,

> some members raised their hands in the air during the music and began shouting and talking in unknown tongues, as described in Mark 16. A few jumped up and down, screaming phrases like "Praise the Lord" and "Hallelujah, precious Jesus. . ." The music continued, and some of the congregation danced and shook uncontrollably. Many communicants focused their attention on snake handling, while others were involved in their own spiritual experience. The young man who first handled the snake passed it to another man. This member began to cry and jump up and down, screaming, "Thank you, Jesus!" The minister took a rattlesnake and placed it on an open Bible that sat on the lectern. The snake immediately coiled, as if it were ready to strike the pastor. The preacher then laid his head on the reptile without being bitten.[15]

Spiritual Otherness on the Margins

Before condemning Serpent Handlers too quickly, we might reflect on certain types of secular "spirituality" such as hang gliding, mountain climbing, and bungee jumping, acts whose devotees often use ecstatic language to describe their life-endangering experiences. Marginalized spirituality is both internal and external, religious experience that, to most, seems eccentric at best, certifiably insane at worst—vision quests that engender strange deeds. Indeed,

69

CHAPTER FOUR

dangerous forms of spirituality often exist in the primal stage of religious movements. Immersion baptism bears inherent life-threatening danger, now rendered symbolic by most congregations. The language of the Lord's Supper—long since softened by Temperance grape juice and the memorialized presence, as opposed to the Real Presence, of Christ in the elements of bread and cup—speaks graphically of life and death, body and blood. Did today's civilized sacraments originate on such spiritual margins?

The Serpent Handlers are small in number, but their rarified approach linking gospel, biblical text, and serpents has made them the focus of studies in both academia and media, which has often facilitated and perpetuated the stereotyping of all Appalachian churches. Nonetheless, their unique interpretation of biblical inerrancy presses that hermeneutic to its limits, as discussed later in this chapter.

PRIMITIVE BAPTIST UNIVERSALISTS: SEEKING THE "HAPPY GOD"

Primitive Baptist Universalists represent another small Appalachian Christian community at the other end of the theological and doctrinal spectrum from Serpent Handlers. Their actions are less life-threatening, but their challenge to Reformation Calvinism may seem no less radical than those who take up serpents.

Jonathan Edwards and the "Angry God"

In a 1741 sermon at a Congregational church in Enfield, Connecticut, Jonathan Edwards, pastor of the Congregational church in Northampton, Massachusetts, declared:

> The God that holds you over the pit of hell, much as one holds a spider, or some loathsome insect over the fire, abhors you, and is dreadfully provoked: His wrath towards you burns like fire; he looks upon you as worthy of nothing else, but to be cast into the fire; he is of purer eyes than to bear to have you in his sight; you are ten thousand times more abominable in his eyes, than the most hateful venomous serpent is in ours. . . . There is no other reason to be given why you have not

70

dropped into hell since you arose in the morning, but that God's hand held you up.[16]

Edwards's words sent such terror into the hearts of his totally depraved audience that he was at times unable to make himself heard over their cries for God's mercy. The Enfield sermon, popularly known as "Sinners in the Hands of an Angry God," is no doubt the most famous and widely circulated sermon Jonathan Edwards ever preached. For decades, it was required reading for high school and college English classes, students less terrified though no less totally depraved, than Edwards's initial hearers. It encapsulates the theology of John Calvin, the sixteenth-century Protestant reformer of Geneva, Switzerland.

Calvin's Reformed theology impacted Primitive Baptists throughout the Appalachian region in the belief that all human beings are totally depraved as a result of the curse of original sin committed by Adam and Eve in the Garden of Eden.

"In Adam's fall we sinned all," the *New England Primer* of 1690 began, teaching the alphabet with biblical soberness.[17] Classic Calvinism asserted that as descendants of Adam, and thus infected with original sin, the human race deserves damnation by a holy God who nonetheless offers some persons unconditional "election" to redemption, an eternal salvation made possible by the sinless sacrifice of Christ whose death and resurrection atoned for the sins of the world. (The elect world, at least.)

Hosea Ballou and A Treatise on Atonement

Not everyone agreed, of course. In 1805, a Calvinist Baptist named Hosea Ballou published *A Treatise on Atonement* in which he asserted that the death of Christ was so overwhelming and overcoming that it provided for the ultimate salvation of all humanity; that sin is punished in this world, not eternity; and that real pleasure was to be found in avoiding sin. In contrast to Edwards, Ballou sought to "happify" the idea of God who, as loving parent, "sent

CHAPTER FOUR

his Son" to redeem the world and return humans to relationship to God like that of the world's first couple.[18]

Ballou reflected the thought of numerous individuals and groups of the seventeenth-century Enlightenment era. His alternative theology would later impact the early Primitive Baptist Universalists.

Primitive Baptist Universalism Takes Shape

Howard Dorgan notes that universalism—the belief that all will be saved—was first institutionalized in Appalachia as early as 1819 with the founding of Consolation Universalist Church in Christian County, Kentucky, followed by the establishment of some twelve Universalist communions in nineteenth-century Kentucky.[19]

Calvinism was carried to the American frontier by eighteenth- and nineteenth-century clergy and laity from Presbyterian, Congregational, and Baptist traditions. Calvinist revival preachers declared the gospel as if everyone could be saved, believing that God would use that word to awaken the elect. Since only God knows who is or is not elected, the preachers "sowed the seed" but God "gave the increase."

As noted earlier in this volume, Primitive Baptists are a specifically Calvinist-oriented denomination that developed among those who advocated the doctrinal tenets of Reformed theology while also resisting "human efforts" to "make Christians" through the use of "unbiblical" means such as Sunday schools, missionary endeavors, Christian colleges, and publishing houses, all futile works of righteousness attempting to usurp the work of the Spirit of God. One early document stated: "We . . . declare a non-fellowship with all such human institutions" and "all societies and traveling beggars for their support, believing them to be the emissaries and agents of antichrist and opposed to the true kingdom of Jesus Christ."[20] Primitive Baptists took that name because they believed that their doctrines came directly from the earliest Christians as passed on through Scripture. In Primitive Baptist theology, sinners do not find God; rather God finds sinners, infusing the grace that makes repentance and faith possible for the totally depraved.

PRIMITIVE BAPTIST UNIVERSALISTS:
AN ALL-INCLUSIVE CALVINISM

By the early twentieth century, however, a small, but fascinating alternative Calvinism appeared among those who came to be known as the Primitive Baptist Universalists (PBUS), colorfully but incorrectly caricatured in Appalachia as "No Hellers." Public knowledge of the PBUS was enhanced with the 1997 publication of a volume entitled *In the Hands of a Happy God: The "No Hellers" of Central Appalachia*, written by the late Howard Dorgan, longtime professor of communications at Appalachian State University. It remains the single most extensive history of the Primitive Baptist Universalists. Dorgan notes that the first public reference to Appalachian Calvinistic universalism seems to come from a 1907 statement in the minutes of the Washington District Primitive Baptist Association in West Virginia. It reads: "Resolved, that whereas, we have been troubled with the doctrine of universalism that we advise the churches that if they have any elders preaching such heresies, or members arguing it, that they admonish them to quit preaching it or talking it, and if they fail to hear them to withdraw fellowship from such."[21]

This was considered the "first admonition" to the PBUS. The full-blown schism within certain Tennessee and Virginia Primitive Baptist regions occurred in 1924; after a series of warnings, the break occurred as specific congregations announced that they were leaving the parent group.

The PBUS believe that the atonement, death, and resurrection of Jesus Christ are so powerful and all-encompassing that all persons will ultimately receive redemption through him. Dorgan lays out the major elements of Primitive Baptist Universalism.

CHAPTER FOUR

- All human beings are sinful; that is the nature of the human condition. Several PBU articles of faith state, "We believe that all mankind is in a fallen state by reason of sin and transgression, and consequently, in a state of condemnation; that man cannot recover himself from that fallen state by his own free will or ability."[22]
- Satan personifies that sinfulness but is only a "natural man" who does not "exist beyond the temporal world."[23]
- Humans cannot escape punishment for their sinful condition, but such punishment occurs in this "temporal world," not in an eternal hell. The appellation "no heller" does not apply, since they believe hell occurs on earth but is not eternal.
- Adam and Eve's sin "irrevocably . . . condemned all humankind to that sinful state of 'natural man,'" thus the atonement of Christ "for the sins of the world" is absolutely necessary.[24]
- Christ's death and resurrection will be applied "for all humankind." Since Adam's sin applied to all humanity, Christ's resurrection will be applied to the entire human race.
- Yet an "elect" does exist and includes Primitive Baptist Universalists and others known only to God, who are "separated from the rest of God's people here in time," and who represent the continued witness of the gospel in the world.
- The elect can and do sin and will be punished by "hell on earth" that purges their sins in this world but not in eternity. The elect's experience of punishment may be greater because of their close relationship with God.
- In the end time, Christ's resurrection will prevail, thereby "paying the price" for all humanity to be redeemed, ending all "sin," "punishment," and "death."
- In that ultimate resurrection, all persons "will go to a wholly egalitarian heaven, the culmination of Christ's universal atonement." The experience of hell on earth will end and only heaven will remain as the eternal abode of the entire human race.[25]

For Primitive Baptist Universalists, hell is a real realm of punishment that reflects an "absence from God's blessing" in the "temporal world."[26] Yet it is not eternal. Life itself is a kind of purgatory in which punishments are dispensed and experienced in this present world. For the Primitive Baptist Universalists it is hell enough right here.

The PBUS are an exceedingly small group, and like most church groups in the United States, they are getting smaller. Dorgan described their geographic boundaries as "northeastern Tennessee, southwestern Virginia, southeastern Kentucky, and southern West Virginia." His initial study suggested that at most there were no more than a thousand members in the churches in the region.[27] They are a religious group born of Appalachia, unashamedly extending the boundaries of salvation to all humanity on the basis of the radically salvific work of Christ on the cross.

Primitive Baptist Universalists reflect a more liberal approach to Christian doctrine, but their churchly practices are classically mountain Baptist. Dorgan, a professor of communications, gives that distinction careful attention, noting five elements he has detected in their homiletical techniques:

- They are extemporaneous; preaching involves the spontaneous inspiration of the Spirit.
- They use "distinctive delivery modes," including "cadence, chant, song, and inflection."
- They reflect the preacher's emotions: "tears, shouts, wails, laughter."
- They are given to great physicality: gestures, "constant movement."
- They reveal a certain "transcendence" reflected in a spiritual state referred to as being "carried out," reflecting a particular type of spirituality in which "God takes control" of both preacher and listeners.[28]

Because so little has been written about the Primitive Baptist Universalists, certain congregational websites provide contemporary

CHAPTER FOUR

voice to their comments and reflections on the nature of their faith. Below are a few examples.

In a documentary film about universalism and PBUs, Elder Jonathan Buttry, of the Holston Primitive Baptist Universalist Church, Rogersville, Tennessee, says:

> Primitive for us means we want to identify with the best of the early Baptist tradition. We want to have freedom of conscience and freedom to question.
>
> If God is omniscient and sovereign, how could any other being thwart his will?
>
> Everything comes from God, and it's going back to God.

Elder Buttry explains that the PBUs are "preterist" in their belief that biblical prophecies regarding the "end times" have already been fulfilled, thus ending speculation as to what they will be in the future.[29]

Elder Reece Maggard, of the same congregation, adds: "God is the father of us all. There's just one blood in this world. We are all a part of him, and if he would lose any part of himself, he'd be losing himself. Because we're a part of his makeup, we're a part of God. That's what people don't see, [they think] God's separated somewhere, that he's way out there somewhere, but it's all right here; right here's where we need him. . . . What's so bad if God is going to save us all? People you thought was friends end up hating you for that."[30]

Primitive Baptist Universalists represent the liberal side of mountain Protestant groups, yet they continue to own their Primitive Baptist origins. They study the Bible and live by its teaching, yet reject the idea of biblical inerrancy and encourage members to explore historical-critical methods in studying the Scripture. They affirm the atonement of Christ for the sins of the world while expanding it from salvation applied only to an elect chosen by God before the foundation of the world; for them, this atonement is so all-sufficient as to produce the ultimate salvation of the human race.

OTHERNESS ON THE MARGINS

SERPENT HANDLERS AND PRIMITIVE
BAPTIST UNIVERSALISTS:
MARGINALIZED SPIRITUALITIES

Serpent Handlers and Primitive Baptist Universalists represent two distinct groups formed in the Appalachian Mountains out of the Holiness-Pentecostal and Primitive Baptist traditions. They are Appalachian minority communions at either end of a theological spectrum. One group demonstrates a deep commitment to the doctrine of biblical inerrancy, evidenced with a powerful, potentially lethal realism. The other distances itself from such a biblical hermeneutic with a sweeping salvific inclusion of the entire human race. Nonetheless, both reflect an expansion of theological interpretations beyond the "orthodox" boundaries of the denominations out of which they came. What may be said of the otherness of their unique and marginalized spiritualities?

Serpent Handlers: Spirituality on the Margins

Whatever else Serpent Handlers represent, they surely point to a spirituality on the margins, the spirituality of otherness, which refuses to be domesticated, often with drastic physical results. Yet such eccentric physical manifestations of the spiritual life are by no means new in Christian history. Below are but a few classic examples:

- *Saint Simeon Stylites.* This hermit monk died in 459 after thirty-seven prayerful years living on a pillar (Greek: *stylos*) in the Syrian desert. Evagrius, the sixth-century historian, wrote of Simeon: "He wore on his body a heavy iron chain. In praying, he bent his body so that his forehead almost touched his feet." Male pilgrims received his counsel; women were forbidden to come near.[31]
- *Saint Francis of Assisi.* Two years before his death in 1226, Saint Francis experienced the stigmata, beginning with a vision that, as his biographer Saint Bonaventure wrote, "left in his heart a wondrous glow, but on his flesh also it imprinted a

77

CHAPTER FOUR

no less wondrous likeness of its tokens. For forthwith there began to appear in his hands and feet the marks of the nails, even as he had just beheld them in that Figure of the Crucified."[32] Francis's stigmata experience was the first of over 300 documented stigmata events that have occurred in church history, many of which endangered the stigmatists' health.

The method of biblical interpretation used by Serpent Handlers is grounded in a belief in biblical inerrancy, a theological commitment that is affirmed by Christians far beyond the Appalachian region. The 1978 Chicago Statement on Biblical Inerrancy provides one of the most widely accepted definitions, including this excerpt from the document's "short statement": "Being wholly and verbally God-given, Scripture is without error or fault in all its teaching, no less in what it states about God's acts in creation, about the events of world history, and about its own literary origins under God, than in its witness to God's saving grace in individual lives."[33]

Those who subscribe to the statement understand it as an affirmation of biblical authority and trustworthiness, essential for interpreting Christian faith and practice to the fullest. It anchors multitudes of Christians in "confirming the word" of God beyond doubt. Yet the high-stakes actions of the Serpent Handlers, which are based on this inerrantist hermeneutic, are a reminder that Christian history is replete with illustrations of ways in which sincere believers have pursued their own form of martyrdom based on a literal reading of the Mark 16 text.

Ralph W. Hood surveys a controversy within the Church of God when serpent handling began in the early twentieth century. He cites the response of Church of God founder and overseer A. J. Tomlinson, based in biblical inerrancy: "And you say that the disciples did not handle serpents? You cannot read of it anywhere in the Bible? I wonder what kind of reader you are. Doesn't the book say that these signs shall follow them that believe, and isn't taking up serpents one of the signs? Were the disciples believers or were they a set of unbelievers?"[34] Hood concludes: "The textual basis of Tomlinson's [1922] analysis is important in illustrating that there is sufficient textual justification for the practices of SHS [serpent-handling sects], and whatever debate one makes textually is an exercise in hermeneutics that cannot be bypassed by refusing to grant the Serpent-Handlers a fair hearing. If extra textual factors are necessary to complete the hermeneutical circle, they apply to the rejection as well as the acceptance of the texts."[35] This assessment suggests that the inerrantist critics of serpent handling cannot have it both ways, claiming the "total authority" of the biblical text, and dismissing two of the five "signs" in Mark 16, three of which continue to be practiced in the larger Holiness-Pentecostal context. It's possible to believe the Bible is inerrant without believing it's always literally true. But the difference may depend on the eye of the believers and the specific inerrancy-based tradition they occupy.

Hood comments: "Pentecostal denominations sought to textually justify a particular expression of emotionality, [namely] *glossolalia*," a reflection that implies evidence of a degree of otherness in the entire movement. He also observes, "Where there is justification for speaking in tongues, there can be justification for handling serpents."[36]

In fact, the Serpent Handlers create a significant hermeneutical problem for those who sign on to the Chicago Statement on Inerrancy whose challenge to practicing the "signs" in Mark 16 seems to be suggesting that the Bible is inerrant except where it isn't.

Primitive Baptist Universalists: Rewriting Reformed Theology

The Primitive Baptist Universalists offer a parallel challenge to Reformed theology. In fact, they come remarkably close to turning it on its head. Calvinism posits the belief that Adam's fall brought total depravity to the entire human race and deserves eternal damnation, yet God's sovereign choice of some individuals for salvation was a gift of God's grace made possible through Jesus Christ. The PBUS acknowledge the race's inherent sinfulness but question the totality of this brokenness as a spiritual condition. They cite the

CHAPTER FOUR.

creation story to suggest that if Adam's fall infected the entire race, then Christ's death and resurrection must redeem the entire race, since he is the "Second Adam."[37]

While PBUS are decidedly more liberal than their traditional Primitive Baptist counterparts, they continue to place their universalism in a Baptist context, with congregational church polity, sacraments of baptism, Holy Communion, and foot washing. PBUS even affirm a doctrine of election, contending that they are elect "witnesses" to Christ's all-embracing salvation. In short, they seek to recapture the benevolent God whose love and grace they find supremely revealed in the incarnation of Jesus of Nazareth.

Therein lies the otherness of their Baptist "witness." They continue to affirm the historic (and biblical) Baptist commitment to a "believers'" church grounded a personal faith in Jesus. They retain the doctrine of divine justice, but limit it to this world. Original sin infects the race but is purged in the here and now. The PBUS take Jesus at his word: "The Kingdom of Heaven is within you," and eventually it will find us all. Primitive Baptist Universalists don't think that's liberal. They think it's gospel.

In distinct but parallel ways, the Serpent Handlers and the Primitive Baptist Universalists reside at the far side of the spirituality of otherness evident in Appalachian Mountain Christianity as sketched out in this text. Both groups demonstrate what Douglas Davies calls "a certain kind of 'inwardness,' a sense of some inner place where we are able to commune with ourselves—that inner place being one that some believers would also see as a meeting place between one's self and otherness."[38] Serpent Handlers understand their spirituality as a direct encounter with the God revealed in Jesus of Nazareth and evidenced in the death-defying ritual whereby "them that believe" win the victory over the serpent (see Mk 16:15–18, KJV). PBUS extend that inwardness ultimately to the entire human race, on the basis of the all-encompassing grace evidenced in Jesus who will not rest until the last "lost sheep" is rescued (see Mt 18:10–14).

OTHERNESS ON THE MARGINS

Yet both of these far-flung theologies grew directly out of mountain Baptist and Holiness-Pentecostal religious traditions long ensconced in the region. In their varied, often contradictory beliefs and practices, these mountain communions also illustrate Douglas Davies's description of a spiritual otherness that includes "beliefs and religious doctrines as part of the values of a society." In their rituals of river baptism, Holy Communion, and the washing of feet; through their preaching styles and conversion experiences, these faith communities illustrate "how sacred texts, rites, and celebrations associated with beliefs become embodied in human feelings, whether in powerful but quickly passing emotions or in influentially enduring moods."[39] This profound spiritual formation, expressed in similar and dissimilar liturgical and doctrinal forms has nurtured Appalachian Christians for generations.

Whether "a certain kind of inwardness" will be sustained, reshaped, or left behind, not only in those mountain Christian traditions but also in faith communities across the religious landscape, is a significant question American churches must confront now and in the years ahead. Perhaps reexamining the nature and practice of that spiritual otherness will provide a helpful starting point. Time and gospel will tell.

NOTES

CHAPTER I.
LOOKING FOR CHRISTIAN APPALACHIA

1. Howard Dorgan, *In the Hands of a Happy God: The "No Hellers" of Central Appalachia* (Knoxville: University of Tennessee Press, 1992), 32–33.

2. "About the Appalachian Region," Appalachian Regional Commission, https://www.arc.gov/about-the-appalachian-region/.

3. "Central Appalachia," The Stay Project, https://www.thestayproject .net/about-central-appalachia#:~:text=Central%20Appalachia%20is%20 the%20heart,Tennessee%20and%20Western%20North%20Carolina.

4. Deborah Vansau McCauley, *Appalachian Mountain Religion: A History* (Urbana: University of Illinois Press, 1995), 1.

5. McCauley, 255.

6. McCauley, 276–310. The term "Holiness" is largely used in mountain churches to refer to congregations with Holiness-Pentecostal spiritual experience and doctrine.

7. McCauley, 1–2.

8. McCauley, 8.

9. Elder John Sparks, *The Roots of Appalachian Christianity: The Life and Legacy of Elder Shubal Stearns* (Lexington: University Press of Kentucky, 2001), xv.

10. Meredith McCarroll, *Unwhite: Appalachia, Race, and Film* (Athens: University of Georgia Press, 2018), 2.

11. McCarroll, 5.

12. McCarroll, 2.

13. Douglas J. Davies, *Emotion, Identity, and Religion: Hope, Reciprocity, and Otherness* (New York: Oxford University Press, 2011), 3.

14. Davies, 3.

NOTES TO CHAPTER ONE

15. Catherine L. Albanese, *America: Religions and Religion*, 3rd ed. (Albany: Wadsworth Publishing Company, 1999), 6.

16. Albanese, 7.

17. Albanese, 341.

18. "Principles of the Gospel Messenger," in *A Sourcebook for Baptist Heritage*, ed. H. Leon McBeth (Nashville: Broadman Press, 1990), 552.

19. "Principles of the Gospel Messenger," 552.

20. "Principles of the Gospel Messenger," 552.

21. "Principles of the Gospel Messenger," 552.

22. "Principles of the Gospel Messenger," 557.

23. Sparks, *The Roots of Appalachian Christianity*, 258.

24. John G. Crowley, *Primitive Baptists of the Wiregrass South: 1815 to the Present* (Gainesville: University Press of Florida, 1998), 60–61.

25. "The Black Rock Address, 1832," in McBeth, *Sourcebook for Baptist Heritage* (Nashville: Broadman Press, 1990), 236.

26. Joshua Guthman, "'Doubts Still Assail Me': Uncertainty and the Making of the Primitive Baptist Self in the Antebellum United States," *Religion and American Culture: A Journal of Interpretation*, 23, no. 1 (Winter 2013): 78.

27. Howard Dorgan, *Giving Glory to God in Appalachia: Worship Practices of Six Baptist Subdenominations* (Knoxville: University of Tennessee Press, 1987), 25.

28. Quote from an Old Regular Baptist in the film *In the Good Old Fashioned-Way*, directed by Herb E. Smith (Whitesburg, Ky.: Appalshop Films, 1972).

29. Crowley, *Primitive Baptists of the Wiregrass South*, 180.

30. Quote from an Old Regular Baptist in the film *In the Good Old Fashioned-Way*.

31. McCauley, *Appalachian Mountain Religion*, 215; Dorgan, *Giving Glory to God in Appalachia*, 59.

32. Dorgan, *In the Hands of a Happy God*, 7.

33. Dorgan, 5.

34. Melvin E. Dieter, "Wesleyan/Holiness Churches," in *Christianity in Appalachia: Profiles in Regional Pluralism*, ed. Bill J. Leonard (Knoxville: University of Tennessee Press, 1999), 228–30.

35. Donald N. Bowdle, "Holiness in the Highlands: A Profile of the Church of God," in Leonard, *Christianity in Appalachia*, 245–46.

36. Kimberly Ervin Alexander, James P. Bowers, and Mark J. Cartledge, "Spirit Baptism, Socialization and Godly Love in the Church of God (Cleveland, TN), *PentecoStudies* 11, no. 1 (2012): 31.

NOTES TO CHAPTERS ONE AND TWO

37. Vershal Hogan, "Church of God Takes on God's Pronouns, Women's Vote at Assembly," FaithonView, July 29, 2022, https://www.faithonview.com/church-of-god-takes-on-gods-pronouns-womens-vote-at-assembly/.

38. Quoted in Frank Macchia, "The Oneness-Trinitarian Pentecostal Dialogue: Exploring the Diversity of Apostolic Faith," *Harvard Theological Review* 103, no. 3: 336–37.

39. McCauley, *Appalachian Mountain Religion*, 7.

40. McCauley, 6–7.

41. Paul Gillespie, ed., *Foxfire 7* (Garden City, N.Y.: Anchor Books, 1982), 69.

42. Francis Beckwith," Bookburning Halloween Celebration at North Carolina Church: Why Didn't I Make the Cut?," *First Things*, October 14, 2009, https://www.firstthings.com/blogs/firstthoughts/2009/10/book-burning-halloween-celebration-at-north-carolina-church-why-didnt-i-make-the-cut.

43. "About Asheville," L. B. Jackson & Co., http://lbjandco.com/about-asheville/; see also Elizabeth Strom and Robert Kerstein, "The Homegrown Downtown: Redevelopment in Asheville, North Carolina," *Urban Affairs Review* 53, no. 3 (2015).

44. Jose Franco, "It's No Easy Trick Being a Witch Today: Many Say Misconceptions Keeping them in the Closet," GoUpstate, October 28, 1999, https://www.goupstate.com/story/news/1999/10/28/it39s-no-easy-trick-being-a-witch-today-many-say-misconceptions-keeping-them-in-the-closet/29615355007/.

45. Ronald D. Eller, *Uneven Ground: Appalachia since 1945* (Lexington: University Press of Kentucky, 2008), 227.

46. "Mountaintop Removal 101," Appalachian Voices, https://appvoices.org/end-mountaintop-removal/mtr101/.

47. McCauley, *Appalachian Mountain Religion*, 189.

48. Helen M. Lewis, "Cherry Log Sermon (2007)", in *Helen Matthews Lewis: Living Social Justice in Appalachia*, ed. Patricia D. Beaver and Judith Jennings (Lexington: University Press of Kentucky, 2012), 208.

49. Lewis, 208–9.

50. Lewis, 210.

CHAPTER 2.
"A HART CHEAREING AND AFFECTING SURMOND"

1. John G. Crowley, *Primitive Baptists in the Wiregrass South: 1815 to the Present* (Gainesville: University Press of Florida, 1998),37.

NOTES TO CHAPTER TWO

2. Crowley, 44.

3. Crowley, 45.

4. Ryan P. Burge, *The Nones, Where They Came From, Who They Are, and Where They Are Going* (Minneapolis: Fortress Press, 2021).

5. David Tracy, *Plurality and Ambiguity: Hermeneutics, Religion and Hope* (San Francisco: Harper & Row, 1987), 9.

6. Tracy, 9.

7. Deborah Vansau McCauley, *Appalachian Mountain Religion: A History* (Urbana: University of Illinois Press, 1995), 17.

8. "Charles Lee, Fire Baptized Holiness Church," in *Foxfire 7*, ed. Paul Gillespie (Garden City: Anchor Books, 1982), 225–26.

9. "Clyde Nations Jr., Ted Laney, and Clyde Nations, Sr., Free Will Baptists," in Gillespie, *Foxfire 7*, 80.

10. William James, *The Varieties of Religious Experience* (New York: The Modern Library, 1902), 163.

11. James, 186.

12. Bill J. Leonard, "Dull Habit or Acute Fever? William James and the Protestant Conversion Crisis," *Harvard Divinity Bulletin* 48, nos. 3–4 (2015): 48.

13. Robert Orsi, "Everyday Miracles: The Study of Lived Religion," in *Lived Religion in America: Toward a History of Practice*, ed. David D. Hall (Princeton: Princeton University Press, 1997), 7.

14. McCauley, *Appalachian Mountain Religion*, 75.

15. Quoted in Elder John Sparks, *The Roots of Appalachian Christianity* (Lexington: University of Kentucky Press, 2001), 65.

16. Sparks, *The Roots of Appalachian Christianity*, 65.

17. Sparks, 69.

18. Deborah McCauley, *Appalachian Mountain Religion*, 83, citing Emma Bell Miles, *The Spirit of the Mountains*, 126.

19. Howard Dorgan, *The Old Regular Baptists of Central Appalachia* (Knoxville: University of Tennessee Press, 1989), 54–55.

20. Dorgan, 55.

21. Dorgan, 57.

22. Dorgan, 57–58.

23. Loyal Jones, *Faith and Meaning in the Southern Uplands* (Urbana: University of Illinois Press, 1999), 109.

24. Jones, 109.

25. James L. Peacock and Ruel W. Tyson Jr., *Pilgrims of Paradox: Cal-*

NOTES TO CHAPTERS TWO AND THREE

vinism and Experience among the Primitive Baptists of the Blue Ridge (Washington, D.C.: Smithsonian Institution Press, 1989), 119.

26. Peacock and Tyson, 122.

27. Peacock and Tyson, 123.

28. Peacock and Tyson, 144.

29. Howard Dorgan, *The Airwaves of Zion: Radio and Religion in Appalachia* (Knoxville: University of Tennessee Press, 1993), 189–90.

30. Dorgan, 122.

31. Ronald D. Eller, *Uneven Ground: Appalachia since 1945* (Lexington: University Press of Kentucky, 2008), 3.

32. Tracy, *Plurality and Ambiguity*, 9.

33. Tracy, 9.

34. McCauley, *Appalachian Mountain Religion*, 189.

35. Crowley, *Primitive Baptists in the Wiregrass South*, 179.

36. Jonathan Edwards, *Religious Affections*, ed. John Smith (New Haven: Yale University Press, 1959), 272.

37. Gillespie, *Foxfire 7*, 64.

38. Jones, *Faith and Meaning*, 133.

39. Jones, 115.

40. *In the Good Old Fashioned-Way*, directed by Herb E. Smith (Whitesburg, Ky.: Appalshop Films, 1972).

41. *In the Good Old Fashioned-Way*.

42. Crowley, *Primitive Baptists in the Wiregrass South*, 112.

43. Crowley, 179.

CHAPTER 3.
REVISITING THE "WOMAN'S SPHERE"

1. Mary Lee Daugherty, *The AMERC Story: An Adventure in Contextual Theological Education* (Berea, Ky.: The Appalachian Ministries Educational Resource Center), 2003.

2. Patricia D. Beaver and Judith Jennings, eds., *Helen Matthews Lewis: Living Social Justice in Appalachia* (Lexington: University Press of Kentucky, 2012.

3. Deborah Vansau McCauley, *Appalachian Mountain Religion: A History* (Urbana: University of Illinois Press, 1995), 62.

4. McCauley, 221.

5. Donald G. Mathews, *Religion in the Old South* (Chicago: University of Chicago Press, 1977), 111.

NOTES TO CHAPTER THREE

6. Mathews, 113.

7. Bill J. Leonard, *Baptists in America* (New York: Columbia University Press, 2005), 208.

8. Christine Leigh Heyrman, *Southern Cross: The Beginnings of the Bible Belt* (New York: Knopf, 1997), 166.

9. Heyrman, 177.

10. Elder John Sparks, *The Roots of Appalachian Christianity: The Life and Legacy of Elder Shubal Stearns* (Lexington: University Press of Kentucky, 2001), 31.

11. Adrienne S. Gaines, "The Church of God Debates Role of Women," *Charisma Magazine*, August 6, 2010, https://charismamag.com/charisma -archive/church-of-god-debates-role-of-women/.

12. Megan Alba, "There Is a Seat at the Table: Affirming Women in Pastoral Ministry," IPHC, General Superintendent's Office, March 10, 2019, https://iphc.org/gso/2019/03/10/there-is-a-seat-at-the-table-affirming -women-in-pastoral-ministry/.

13. Bob Allen, "Southern Baptist Leader Questions Moderates' Credibility on Women's Ordination," Good Faith Media, August 22, 2006, https://goodfaithmedia.org/southern-baptist-leader-questions-moderates -credibility-on-womens-ordination-cms-7793/.

14. Marv Knox, "Southern Baptist Convention Ousts Its Largest Church," *Baptist News Global*, February 21, 2023, https://baptistnews.com /article/southern-baptist-convention-ousts-its-largest-church-saddleback -for-having-a-woman-pastor/.

15. "Articles of Faith," Baptist Bible Fellowship International, https:// www.bbfi.org/articles-of-faith.

16. Jeff Todd Titon, *Powerhouse for God: Speech, Chant and Song in an Appalachian Baptist Church* (Austin: University of Texas Press, 1988), 141–42.

17. Howard Dorgan, *The Old Regular Baptists of Central Appalachia: Brothers and Sisters in Hope* (Knoxville: University of Tennessee Press, 1989), 43–44.

18. Howard Dorgan, *In the Hands of a Happy God: the "No-Hellers" of Central Appalachia* (Knoxville: University of Tennessee Press, 1997), 124.

19. Dorgan, *The Old Regular Baptists of Central Appalachia*, 239.

20. Rosemary Radford Ruether and Rosemary Skinner Keller, *Women and Religion in America*, vol. 3, *1900–1968* (San Francisco: Harper & Row Publishers, 1986), 260–261.

21. Helen M. Lewis and Monica Appleby, *Mountain Sisters: From Convent to Community in Appalachia* (Lexington: University Press of Kentucky, 2003), 6.

NOTES TO CHAPTERS THREE AND FOUR

22. Lewis and Appleby, xxi.

23. Lewis and Appleby, 68.

24. Lewis and Appleby, 72.

25. "Eve Is Again Listening to the Voice of the Serpent," Landmark Independent Baptists Church, https://www.libcfl.com/articles/woman.ht; Leonard, *Baptists in America*, 222.

CHAPTER 4.
OTHERNESS ON THE MARGINS

1. Deborah Vansau McCauley, *Appalachian Mountain Religion: A History* (Urbana: University of Illinois Press, 1995),107–9.

2. David Tracy, *Plurality and Ambiguity: Hermeneutics, Religion, Hope* (San Francisco: Harper & Row, 1987), 9.

3. Tracy, 9.

4. Cambridge Dictionary, s.v. "dissent," accessed January 2, 2024, https://dictionary.cambridge.org/dictionary/english/dissent.

5. Edwin Scott Gaustad, *Dissent in American Religion* (Chicago: University of Chicago Press, 1973),

6. Gaustad, 4–5.

7. Gaustad, 4.

8. See "The Longer Ending of Mark," in *The New Oxford Annotated Bible*, ed. Bruce M. Metzger and Roland E. Murphy (New York: Oxford University Press, 1991), 74–75n.

9. Bill J. Leonard, "Leave Your Medicine Outside," in *After the Genome: A Language for Our Biotechnological Future*, ed. Michael J. Hyde and James A. Herrick (Waco, Tex.: Baylor University Press, 2013), 131.

10. Eleanor Dickinson and Barbara Benziger, *Revival!* (San Francisco: Harper & Row), 127–28; Bill J. Leonard, "The Bible and Serpent-Handling," in *Perspectives on American Religion and Culture*, ed. Peter W. Williams (Oxford, UK: Blackwell Publishers, 1999), 228.

11. Ralph W. Hood Jr., "When the Spirit Maims and Kills: Social Psychological Considerations of the History of Serpent Handling Sects and the Narrative of Handlers," *International Journal for the Psychology of Religion*, 8, no. 2 (1998): 71.

12. Thomas Burton, *Serpent-Handling Believers* (Knoxville: University of Tennessee Press, 1993), 134.

13. Mary Lee Daugherty, "Serpent-Handling as Sacrament," *Theology Today* 33, no. 3 (1976): 232–43.

NOTES TO CHAPTER FOUR

14. "Despite Pastor's Death, Followers Are Still Handling Snakes," CBS News, February 26, 2014, https://www.cbsnews.com/news/despite-pastors-death-followers-are-still-handling-snakes/.

15. David L. Kimbrough, *Taking Up Serpents: Snake Handlers of Eastern Kentucky* (Chapel Hill: University of North Carolina Press, 1995), 18.

16. Jonathan Edwards, "Sinners in the Hands of an Angry God," in *Jonathan Edwards: Representative Selections*, ed. Clarence H. Faust and Thomas H. Johnson (New York: Hill and Wang, 1962), 164.

17. *The New England Primer* (Boston, 1690), https://www3.nd.edu/~rbarger/www7/neprimer.html.

18. Howard Dorgan, *In the Hands of a Happy God: The "No Hellers" of Central Appalachia* (Knoxville: University of Tennessee Press, 1997), 105–6.

19. Dorgan, 112.

20. John G. Crowley, *Primitive Baptists of the Wiregrass South* (Gainesville: University Press of Florida, 1998), 60.

21. Dorgan, *In the Hands of a Happy God*, 51.

22. Dorgan, 90.

23. Dorgan, 5.

24. Dorgan, 5.

25. Dorgan, 5.

26. Dorgan, 89.

27. Dorgan, 6.

28. Dorgan, 128. The Tennessee-based Holston Primitive Baptist Universalist Church reflects a more lecture-like approach to preaching, as evidenced in this video. "Holston-A Primitive Baptist Universalist Church," streamed live on September 11, 2022, Facebook video, https://www.facebook.com/watch/live/?ref=watch_permalink&v=618955873275814.

29. "What Is Primitive Baptist Universalism?," from *Love Unrelenting*, by Steven Hause, February 6, 2022, YouTube video, https://www.youtube.com/watch?v=rZgqYZPrMlo.

30. "What Is Primitive Baptist Universalism?" The Holston PBU church seems to be the only or primary such congregation to broadcast its Sunday services and group discussions. The church makes clear its liberal viewpoints.

31. Evagrius, *Ecclesiastical History*, bk. 1, ch. 13, https://sourcebooks.fordham.edu/source/evagrius-simeon.asp.

32. Saint Bonaventure, *The Life of Saint Francis of Assisi*, trans. E. Gurney Salter (New York: E.P. Dutton, 1904), ch. 13, https://www.ecatholic2000.com/bonaventure/assisi/francis.shtml.

33. International Council on Biblical Inerrancy, "The Chicago State-

NOTES TO CHAPTER FOUR

ment on Biblical Inerrancy" (1978), https://www.etsjets.org/files/documents /Chicago_Statement.pdf.

34. Ralph W. Hood Jr., "When the Spirit Maims and Kills: Social Psychological Considerations of the History of Serpent Handling Sects and the Narrative of Handlers," *International Journal for the Psychology of Religion* 8, no. 2 (1998): 80–81.

35. Hood, 81.

36. Hood, 75.

37. Dorgan, *In the Hands of a Happy God*, 91.

38. Douglas J. Davies, *Emotion, Identity, and Religion: Hope, Reciprocity, and Otherness* (New York: Oxford University Press, 2011), 3.

39. Davies, 3.

INDEX

Albanese, Catherine, 6–7
Amazing Grace Baptist Church, 19
Appalachian Ministries
    Educational Resource Center,
    45, 68–69
Appalachian Regional
    Commission, 2
Appleby, Monica, 57

Ballou, Hosea, 71–72
Baptist Bible Fellowship, 53
Baptists: "No Heller," 64–64;
    Primitive Baptist Universalists,
    11, 63–70; Southern Baptist
    Convention, 2, 52–53. *See also*
    Old Regular Baptists; Primitive
    Baptists
Berea College, 36, 42, 45
Brasher, John Larkin, 36
Bridges, Linda McKinnish, 3,
    61–62
Burton, Tom, 68
Buttry, Jonathan, 76

Calvin, John, 8, 71, 73
Calvinism, 8, 29, 31, 65, 71–72
Chicago Statement on Biblical
    Inerrancy, 78

Church of God (Anderson, Ind.),
    12
Church of God (Cleveland, Tenn.),
    12, 51
Complementarity, 51–56
Cooper, Wallace, 1
Crowley, John G., 11, 25, 41, 45

Daugherty, Mary Lee, 47, 68–69
Davies, Douglas J., 6, 81
Davis, Addie, 52
Dollar, Creflo, 18
Dorgan, Howard, 3–4, 16, 21, 29, 33,
    40–41, 49

Edwards, Jonathan, 41–42, 70–77,
    79–80
Edwards, Morgan, 34
Eller, Ron, 21, 39

Fire-Baptized Holiness Church,
    29, 55
Foxfire 7, 16, 41
Francis of Assisi, 77–78

Gaustad, Edwin Scott, 65–66
Glenmary Sisters, 56–58
Guthman, Joshua, 9

INDEX

Hall, Eula, 23
Holiness-Pentecostals, 12–14, 49, 66
Hood, Ralph W., 68, 78–79

In the Good Old Fashioned-Way, 43

Jakes, T. D., 18
James, William, 30
Jesus Only Pentecostals, 14–15;
    Oneness Pentecostals, 14
Johns, Sheryl Bridges, 51

Kimbrough, David, 69

Lewis, Helen, 23, 47

Maggard, Reece, 76
Marshall, Daniel, 34, 50
Marshall, Marsha Stearns, 50–51
McCarroll, Meredith, 5
McCauley, Deborah Vansau, 1–4,
    16, 21–22, 29, 33, 40, 48–49

"No Heller" Baptists, 64–65

Old Regular Baptists, 7–8, 10–11,
    19–20, 37, 43, 54
Orsi, Robert, 33
Osteen, Joel and Victoria, 18
Otherness/Othering, 5–6, 22, 29,
    39, 61–62, 64, 66, 69, 77, 80–81

Parham, Howard, 16–17, 41
Pentecostals, 1–2, 8–10; Holiness-
    Pentecostals, 12–14, 49, 66;
    Jesus Only Pentecostals, 14–15;
    Oneness Pentecostals, 14
Preast, Elzie, 68
Primitive Baptists, 1, 7, 11, 19–20,
    37, 73–77, 89, 90n28, 90n30
Primitive Baptist Universalists, 11,
    63–70

Reuther, Rosemary Radford, 47
Rice, John R., 55–56

Saddleback Valley Church, 55
Serpent Handlers / Serpent
    handling, 63–70, 77–80
Simeon Stylites, 77
Southern Baptist Convention, 2,
    52–53
Sparks, John, 4, 34, 50–51
Stay Project, 2
Stearns, Shubal, 34, 50
Surgener, Lydia, 45–46, 48–49

Tomlinson, A. J., 78
Tracy, David, 28, 40, 65

Wake Forest University School of
    Divinity, 27, 30
Woman's sphere, 50, 56

GEORGE H. SHRIVER LECTURE SERIES IN
RELIGION IN AMERICAN HISTORY

1 *Religion and the American Nation: Historiography and History*,
by JOHN F. WILSON

2 *The Protestant Voice in American Pluralism*,
by MARTIN E. MARTY

3 *The Creation-Evolution Debate: Historical Perspectives*,
by EDWARD J. LARSON

4 *Religion Enters the Academy:
The Origins of the Scholarly Study of Religion in America*,
by JAMES TURNER

5 *The Faiths of the Postwar Presidents: From Truman to Obama*,
by DAVID L. HOLMES

6 *Urban Origins of American Judaism*,
by DEBORAH DASH MOORE

7 *Of Gods and Games: Religious Faith and Modern Sports*,
by WILLIAM J. BAKER

8 *An Uncommon Faith:
A Pragmatic Approach to the Study of African American Religion*,
BY EDDIE S. GLAUDE JR.

9 *Southern Religion in the World: Three Stories*,
bY PAUL HARVEY

10 *Appalachian Mountain Christianity: The Spirituality of Otherness*,
bY BILL J. LEONARD

Printed in the United States
by Baker & Taylor Publisher Services